Susie Orbach is a psychotherapist and writer. She co-founded The Women's Therapy Centre and Antidote, the organisation promoting emotional literacy and is a visiting Professor at the LSE. Her most recent book is *The Impossibility of Sex*.

Other Books by Susie Orbach

Fat is a Feminist Issue
Fat is a Feminist Issue II
Hunger Strike:
The Anorectic's Struggle as a Metaphor of our Age
The Impossibility of Sex

and with Luise Eichenbaum

Understanding Women:
A Feminist Psychoanalytic Account
What Do Women Want?:
Exploding The Myth of Dependency
Between Women
Love, Competition and Envy in Women's
Relationships

What's Really Going On Here?

Susie Orbach

A *Virago* Book

First published by Virago Press 1994

Reprinted 1994, 1995, 1996, 1999

This collection and introduction copyright © Susie Orbach 1984

The moral right of the author has been asserted

A CIP catalogue record for this book
is available from the British Library

ISBN 1 85381 798 8

Printed and bound in Great Britain by Clays Ltd, St Ives plc

Virago
A Division of
Little, Brown and Company (UK)
Brettenham House
Lancaster Place
London WC2E 7EN

For Lukie, Lianna, Gudrun and Joseph

Contents

Contents

Acknowledgements

Many many thanks to Roger Alton, Nicola Stockton, Duncan Campbell, Deborah Orr and Helen Oldfield at the *Guardian*. To Joseph Schwartz for being prepared to read, criticise kindly and sub every column on demand. To Caroline Pick for understanding the point of the project. To Sally Berry who never forgets to tell me she has read them. To Petra Fried for help on many fronts. To Caradoc King for his enthusiasm. To Lennie Goodings for her efforts to get into my head and edit sensitively. To Gillian Slovo, for our sustaining daily 'cup of coffee'.

Introduction

The opportunity to write a regular column for *Guardian Weekend* answered a long-brewing desire of mine to address, in a public forum, aspects of the interpenetration of private, civic and political life.

All around us we see a society bursting at the seams with its failure to meet people's needs. These failures are expressed in graphic outbursts of violence, reflecting widespread personal despair and despondency. Our social relations are saturated with violence – from the racist thugs in London's East End, to the Saturday football hooligans, to the routine bullying of school-children. In the domestic sphere the extent of violence between men and women, and the sexual battering of infants, small children and women appalls us. And yet, while we have many theories that talk about the economic and social roots of crowd fanaticism and sexual violence, they fail to take account of how we shape emotional life in such a way that social violence, perverse social relations and distorted interpersonal relationships are endemic.

Through the lens of emotion, I've wanted to bring into focus meanings of the often bizarre, destructive, chaotic, private and public behaviours around us; to make sense of the pain, anguish, aggravation and hurt that characterise so much of our interior lives, and to suggest ways of reframing our experiences – political and personal – that might move us beyond senseless repetition.

My project, in its broadest possible sense, is to address the emotional illiteracy that has become our way of life – a form of ignorance that envelops us so pervasively that, like the force of gravity, we are often unaware of it. We act from it without much cognizance or examination. By upholding the cultural and private values about restricting our emotions that we have assimilated into our codes for living, we relegate an understanding or facility with emotional life to the periphery of conscious experience. We consider feelings to be a stuff-and-nonsense irrelevance, a mystery, or a fearful genie which, once released, will never return to the safe confines of its internal bottle.

Our literary, filmic, artistic and musical endeavours illustrate the drawing power of strong, even exaggerated, emotions through the Romance, the Western, the Horror story, the Adventure, the Thriller and the Drama. But curiously, the emotional base that motivates all art and makes it alive for so many people is, in daily life, trivialised, avoided and feared.

We place a high value on the repression of feeling. The phrases 'Grin and bear it', 'Keep a stiff upper lip', 'Don't be such a baby', 'She's just winding you up', and 'Pull yourself together' express the routine mandates that corset our emotional terrain. These apparently innocent prescriptions for survival attempt to describe and constrain emotional life. But unlike a corset – a piece of clothing we can discard when the situation calls for it – this constraint hampers, in the deepest possible way, a person's ability to develop fully, to know themselves, to know what they are feeling and what they are wanting. When we are unclear about our emotional state we are compelled to act unconsciously. Somnolent to awareness we distort our potential. Instead, we can be destructive, chaotic and capricious.

Emotional illiteracy produces a divide between the private

and public worlds, as though these realms of experience can be neatly shorn off one from another. But even if we fail to emotionally register what happens in public policy, it nevertheless deeply affects us. Just as what occurs in the privacy of our relationships affects what we bring to society as a whole.

Because emotions embarrass and alarm us we replace them with romance, nostalgia and heroism. These are the public and quasi-acceptable poles of the expression of feelings. While we can comfortably cry at a wedding, poignantly remember a piece of history that is safely tucked away, and applaud courage on the sports field or in the back of an ambulance, assimilation into British culture means learning to contain and suppress the wide range of ordinary, everyday emotional expression. But even in those cultures known for their exuberant show of emotion – Mediterraneans, Jews, Caribbeans, Africans, North and South Americans, and so on – the display of emotion is not analogous to emotional literacy. The problem of emotional illiteracy, while perhaps most visible in Southern Britain, is almost universal in westernised societies.

Our discomfort with emotions makes them low priority. In the old adage, health precedes wealth which precedes happiness. But relegated as it is to third position, the attainment of happiness becomes less of a goal and more of a wistful desire, and happiness itself becomes abstracted and idealised. Happiness is often conceived of as a state hermetically sealed off from difficult feelings. But like a sauce that tastes too thin when the stock has been left out, where layers of reduced and concentrated flavours that need to liaise together have been replaced by artificial additives, happiness, cut off from the digestion of our other feelings, is synthetic. We need to learn the grammar of the psyche and its emotions, to develop a fluency with them, so we can extend our emotional vocabulary, without which happiness is a hollow shell.

The articles collected here attempt to extend this vocabulary and to name experiences in the language of human emotions. By setting everyday emotions such as love, jealousy and anger in social and political contexts, I have tried to show the interrelatedness of the public and the private. I have then tried to explore the internal pathways the psyche takes to manage pain or hurt of one kind or another. In the broader political pieces in Section 1, I have attempted to question the emotional and political impact of public policy and political events on us, both as individuals and collectively. I've suggested that the limited ways in which we frame political discussion inhibits our capacity to act as citizens.

Throughout the book, I have sometimes reflected on the experiences of the individual (Sections 2 and 3), sometimes on those of the couple (Section 4), sometimes on those between parent and child (Section 3), and sometimes on those of women (Section 5). The attempt is to dignify and to clarify the authorship of individual or group responses so that we understand some of what motivates bullying, for example, or underlines the appeal of romance. Much of psychology unwittingly blames or excuses away people's behaviours. But I have hoped to show here the agency, the logic, the 'what people are trying to do' behind the individual and collective acts that can often seem incomprehensible or irrational.

In psychotherapy understandings are developed over a long period of time. There is no such thing as a complete or permanent interpretation, rather a set of provisional understandings that analyst and analysand make in their endeavour together. When these provisional understandings are insufficient they create new ones.

These articles, by contrast, are by their very nature frozen in print. They are psychic snapshots, reflecting a set of understandings at a given moment. They are not comprehensive or exhaustive, but attempts at opening up new ways of seeing and thinking about psychic dilemmas. My hope is to open a dialogue with the reader, rather than offer highly elaborated, polished understandings that can often explain away situations, rather than leaving them open for the continuing improvement in understanding that must occur if they are to help foster real change. They are as much aimed at the reader who may be sceptical about the place of emotion in public and private life, as to the reader who already has a confirmed interest in such a project.

My wider project is to create an emotionally literate culture, where the facility to handle the complexities of emotional life is as widespread as the capacity to read, write and do arithmetic. Emotional literacy is not about the public confessional à la the Oprah Winfrey Show. It is not about therapy as a spectator sport. Nor is it about psychobabble. Emotional literacy is about making it possible to ask the question 'How are you?' and to be able to hear the reply. It is about hearing another's distress without being impelled to smother their feelings; about allowing the complexity of our emotional responses to co-exist without commandeering them into simplified categories of good and bad; about finding a way to accept the differences between us without resorting to prejudice or emotional fundamentalism. Emotional literacy is about observing our political responses before we slot them into jingoism, or the gut-checking guilt that can paralyse thought. Emotional literacy is a call for a new agenda in which we restructure our institutions to accommodate and enhance our emotional, social and civic selves. Emotional literacy is about recognising the importance of our emotional life in all aspects of our lives.

Susie Orbach
London, 1993

Towards Emotional Literacy in Public and Private Life

Emotional illiteracy exists because we have no shared language for emotional life. Words like love, hate, jealousy and competition reveal little more than the tip of an emotional experience whose depths we are unused to exploring.

Emotional Literacy

We live in a culture that imposes a great dichotomy between our private lives and our public lives; our inner lives and our outer lives. Yet our public and private worlds have much in common. To both we bring deep personal aspirations, our hopes for fulfilment, for connection, for expressiveness. But both worlds are fraught. Our hopes are punctured by denial, disappointment, frustration and cruelty.

Behind closed doors countless instances of horrific child abuse and wife battering are occuring. We hear of marriages gone dreadfully wrong, of alcoholic fathers and mothers, of drug-crazed teenage children. We see racist yobs roaming the cities, runaway kids sleeping rough, doss-house men and shopping-bag ladies.

Everywhere around us is evidence of emotional brutality to self and other. The search for connection and the drive to obliterate it is so commonplace that we scarcely notice or register it. We are passively complicit. We feel powerless to intervene when the boys hit each other in the playground: 'boys will be boys'; we close our ears to the merciless teasing of one girl by three others.

What I am describing is the phenomenon of emotional illiteracy. The institutions which shape our experience from the cradle to the grave unwittingly brutalise the personal. Our emotional needs get exploited rather than addressed. We reward ourselves for achievement, for managing everything, for not collapsing, and, most fundamentally of all, for not needing.

Emotional illiteracy affects every aspect of our culture. Reflect on the following two unremarkable everyday examples.

The parent unpeeling herself from the child snivelling at the nursery door not wanting to be left tries to humour the child by denying the pain of the separation and saying: 'What a little actress you are.' But in this denial of the child's momentary anguish and in the parent's sense of the child winding her or him up, we negate the experiences of the child and adult, and in doing so deny both of them a feeling of authenticity.

We can't bear to see the child's (albeit short-lived) distress. We feel impelled to shrug it off; to deny; to make nice. As the beleaguered adult whose child inside was similarly denied, whose adult life may be less supported than we wish, we repress our own pain and bid our children do the same. We can barely imagine both acknowledging the distress ('Yes, it is sad to say goodbye') and continuing with our plan to leave the child. We are fearful lest recognition of the child's wish not to be left will dissuade us from the task we have to help our children and ourselves with – the task of separation.

But the pain (and the excitement) of separation is best dealt with – as are all feelings – when they can be recognised and acknowledged. To recognise a feeling is not, as so many fear, to succumb to it, to be driven by it, to be in its sway. Recognition allows us to experience it directly, digest it and – as it were – be done with it. We can hug the child wholeheartedly, receive her distress and give her a hopeful send-off.

In order to do this we need to face our own feelings about saying goodbye to the child. We may feel sad, we may feel relieved, we may remember the sorrow or pleasure of being left ourselves at that age. Whatever we are feeling – and we are bound to be experiencing a complex of emotions – the feelings are there whether we acknowledge them or not. The more we can accept our emotional states, the less we are driven by them, the less scared and seemingly irrational is our behaviour.

A man loves a woman desperately but cannot bear his need for her. It makes him feel weak. One day he is driven into a jealous fury when she is late home and is shocked to find himself hitting her. The fear and contempt of his own dependency, which he tries so hard to conceal from himself, turns into a hatred towards her – the object of his need. Unable to acknowledge his need but unable to keep it inside himself any longer, it explodes outside his body. His anger hides the fearful feeling, circumvents the recognition of his need, pushes the woman away and threatens the relationship.

He doesn't know why he hits out, why he feels impelled to reject the person he loves. He doesn't know that her lateness produced in him terrifying feelings of abandonment which no one has ever helped him come to terms with in his life. Feelings of abandonment, feelings of emotional need terrify him. He has created a shield against knowing that he is experiencing those feelings. In time, the shield against these hidden inner feelings becomes a weapon that he can't control.

Emotional illiteracy exists because we have no shared language for emotional life. Words like love, hate, jealousy and competition reveal little more than the tip of an emotional experience whose depths we are unused to exploring.

When we try to talk about our feelings directly ('How are you today?' 'Pretty awful actually.' 'Never mind, cheer up, luv, can't be all terrible.') we both feel and engender shame and embarrassment. When we try to create a new language, a way of telling, we face scorn for speaking psychobabble. But while it's true that psychobabble is an ugly and cheap way to solve the problems of putting inchoate feelings into words, it's also true that the scorn expresses our culture's fear of the emotional. Language for many of us has been a way of hiding our feelings from ourselves, and a way of not disclosing them to others.

What we are wanting and seeking in our relationships – both public and private – is recognition, emotional connection and a chance to understand and express the deepest parts of our self. In our private world we long for the reparative powers of emotional authenticity even as we fear it will render us too vulnerable.

The emotional connections we crave need to inform our cultural practices. It is well nigh time that we thought through the emotional requirements demanded in pre- and post-natal settings so that parents have a place to explore the emotional meanings of parenting; in our nurseries so that children's emotional development – their subjective experience – gets as much attention as their social skills; in our schools so that curiosity is not hampered by emotional problems brought from home or encountered in the playground or with authority in general; in our political parties so that they can become a real forum for ideas, policies and feelings rather than a place of display and alienation; in our workplaces so that co-operation can replace rivalry and competition. The list could go on and on, because emotional illiteracy is endemic.

We need to challenge our culturally transmitted fear of emotions. A fear of emotions exploits and distorts people's longings and desires. A fear of emotions curtails our health, our marriages, our relationships with children as well as our capacity for citizenship. Until we challenge the consensus that keeps us emotionally illiterate, our desire for recognition, for intimacy, for selfhood and for community will continue to appear in fragmented, distorted forms.

War Tests Our Mental Health

'My daughter aged 9 has been having nightmares all week about chemical warfare. How can I calm her properly when I am having the same nightmares myself?'

There can't be many of us who haven't had to cope with the psychological impact of the Gulf war in our waking and sleeping hours. The night-time start of the war added to a feeling of instability. We went to sleep hearing the latest reports and woke up wondering what on earth had happened in the night. While our children may have been spared the late-night news reports and the anxiety they unleashed, children are bound to pick up the worry and concern all around them. How should we handle this? What is a proper response, one that will neither frighten them further nor push them into a state of denial?

In order to help our children, we – parents, teachers, nursery school workers, childminders, nannies, au pairs and babysitters – need to be able to engage with the *emotional* impact that war has on us. Often our political responses, valid and crucial as they indeed are, become vested with the difficult emotional realities we find hard to face. But it is important that we allow those emotional realities into our awareness directly.

War in any circumstances renders one extremely vulnerable and powerless. And if one is a spectator (as almost all of us in the UK are of most wars) the feelings of vulnerability and powerlessness have little chance to be converted into another form such as heroism, caring for others, healing the wounded and so on. Vulnerability is not an emotion we in this culture are very good at coping with. We've developed all sorts of protective mechanisms to distance ourselves from it so that when these feelings come crashing in on us we may find ourselves ill-equipped to handle them. Feelings of vulnerability caused by the Gulf war meet in our unconscious a basic form of vulnerability we experienced early on in our psychological development which we may have dealt with by splitting it off and repressing it. We can become extremely frightened, not simply because a war far from home renders us as individuals small and somewhat impotent, but because we are encountering several complex psychological phenomena at the same time.

On the one hand we are trying to think about the unthinkable. To digest the meaning of carpet bombing, of the ability of humanity to create weapons of enormous destruction, and to use them. We know the tragedy the loss of one human life causes but the psyche finds it extremely hard to emotionally absorb reports of 'minor fatalities'. The terms 'minor' and 'fatalities' in this context serve to sanitise both the act of killing and the impact of death. For these are almost too hard to hold in mind, to think about, to bear emotionally.

On the other hand, we are battling internally with the mechanisms of repression we've relied on to quiet a basic insecurity many of us feel. When these mechanisms creak under the weight of what is now demanding repression, we become fearful, fearful not just of war, but fearful that our ways of managing vulnerability will leak and we will be swamped by dreadful feelings of powerlessness.

A third factor relates to destructiveness. Within us all is the capacity for love, generosity, concern and care. And within us all is the capacity for aggression, anger, rage and humiliation. As a culture we find such emotions difficult, uncomfortable. We both admire and abhor aspects of their expression in others while we try to keep a lid on the expression of such feelings ourselves. When the world and our leadership go to war in our name (whether we agree with the war or dispute its necessity) our conflicting feelings about our individual potential for violence and destructiveness is stimulated and we may have a very confusing set of responses to reports of targets 'successfully hit'. We may find ourselves excited as though our own destructive feelings are being gratified and then hastily appalled as we allow into consciousness the awareness that ordinary and military people, countries and ecological balances are being destroyed.

The combination of these complex psychological phenomena makes for a sticky stew when we try to relate to our children. A common way we get out of it is through a resort to moralism, nationalism or jingoism. If we can make what is going on in our name sound right then the uncomfortable bits, the feelings of vulnerability, of powerlessness, the encounter with our own destructive feelings, our difficulty with absorbing the idea of death, can slip from consciousness and we can feel a sense of relief. But this relief can only be temporary for it requires constant recharging to bind up these extremely complex phenomena. Even if we do support the war, the feelings I've discussed still need to be faced lest they lead us into blind support for military command.

But of course the situation is not so simple. Roughly half the British population declared their disapproval of military intervention in the Gulf. And yet this opposition, unlike that in Germany, France and the United States, is not that visible. This intensifies the psychological distress of feelings of powerlessness, of violation, of the negation of the exercise of citizenship, of invisibility, of individual outrage. Joined with the complex of feelings I have already discussed, this is an awful lot to hold on to.

So to turn back now to the children. What is to be done? How can we help them with their feelings?

There is a widespread sense (from schools, psychologists, analysts) that children deal with war through denial. I think many do, but need they and should they, and how long can denial be viable?

We are accustomed to thinking that children can only cope with things portrayed in terms of good and bad; that their moral sense is entwined with their emotional development in such a way that they cope with fear by converting it into hating the baddies while gathering strength by identifying with the goodies. But this characterisation of kids infantilises them and us.

Many children experience enormous relief in talking about war. They pick up images from the TV. These images join with images of fighting from children's TV programmes, but now they sense the gravity and concern in their parents. So they sense that this fighting is different, not fantastical. How scared should they be? How can we soothe them? Can children cope with a scenario not cleanly divided into goodies and baddies?

If we can begin to tolerate the complexities of our own feelings, we stand a very good chance of helping children deal with their fears directly. We can help them with the feelings of powerlessness and confusion by allowing them to give voice to them – not immediately reassuring them or shushing them. We would do well to let them talk about war, ask questions and discuss it; draw and write about it. Our ability to engage with their curiosity and their feelings will remove that extra layer of fear. They don't need to be frightened of having frightening feelings. We can acknowledge that war makes us feel scared without it meaning that we are shaken to our roots. And perhaps we can help them socialise their responses as did one New York City school. Teachers of the 7- to 10-year-olds held a forum to air thoughts and feelings about the Gulf war following a homework assignment in which the pupils were to write down how they felt about war; how someone else in their household felt about war; what they thought the war was about;

what the different positions were. I end with a letter from two little girls:

Dear Mr President Bush;
How are you? We are 7. But we think that the war is not necessary. We think that the money for the war should be used for homes for the homeless. Please, we're scared. You may not listen but give it a thought.
from
Gina and Hunter,
Manhattan County School
New York City

On Shaky Moral Ground

Talk of morals, morality and moral values largely focuses on the imperative of morality rather than the meaning of morality. While theologians have attempted to raise the issue of the meaning of morality, the government insists that the talk be of teaching morality.

In the wake of the killing of 2-year-old Jamie Bulger by children only just 10 years old, in the aftermath of ghastly revelations about practices in children's homes, psychiatric hospitals and old people's homes, where those in charge desperately fail those they are meant to care for; from the evidence we have about the rise in crime and the disregard for law, teachers are now being mandated to instil in their pupils moral values – the learning of right from wrong – as though these endeavours were somehow well out of step with what is part of teaching anyway.

Few of us would want to dissuade teachers from acting as agents in the discourse of morality. For many teachers, pedagogics is a deeply moral act; an expression of faith. One teaches in order to help children become conscious, to extend their curiosity and to develop the skills so that they have the capacity to enter and influence society with their values. But education now is being seriously retooled. Instead of learning and thinking for all, we are supposed to accommodate ourselves to a shrinking economy, fewer opportunities and the reinstallation of a class system in which there are those who have access to learning and further education and those who have very much more limited possibilities.

None of what I am saying is new. We all recognise this retooling in education, in health care, in housing, in mental health services, in transportation, in access to cultural activities, sports and so on. What is novel in the situation is the government's exhortation in what, from my perspective is an 'immoral' climate, to shape up as a culture and act 'moral'. While the very things that bind us together as a culture – in big and small ways, in our local communities and in our wider sense of ourselves as a society – are being dismantled by the government, we are scolded for our lack of values. Shouldn't we rather examine what is causing the breakdown and despair behind the destructive behaviour we witness?

Morals are important. Shared values are important. A culture knows itself through its commonly held values, beliefs and practices. We belong to or are alienated from our community based upon our acceptance or rejection of communal ideas about how to live and what is important. But there is a difference between the exhortation to hold certain values, and the collective and individual belief in them. Different communities create different value systems. There is no such thing as a moral value *per se*; there are only competing values which vie for ascendancy, and in the struggle for dominance of a particular set of values the deployment of the word 'moral' is used to silence difference, to bind up difficulty, to keep problematic ideas in check, through the mechanism of conscience.

A call for morality is a simplistic way to demand that people conform to received ideas of 'right' and 'wrong' rather than exploring and understanding the meaning of differing values and the difficulties that beset us as individuals and as a society.

In acting 'moral' on command, we give up the vibrancy that comes of tackling difficulty, of arriving at a position through reflection, of learning how to tolerate conflicting desires. We bind up the conflict through the coercing weight of 'morality' and in so doing we deprive ourselves of the opportunity to understand what we are striving for, what our beliefs mean, why they motivate us. Morality from this perspective has the same meaning as rote-learning the 'three Rs'. We don't learn about the magic of numbers, about the relationships between numbers, through memorising our times tables. If we are lucky and don't get turned off, then our tables provide us with a technical device that might allow us to explore the pleasure of numerical relations. We learn our tables as a grammar with which to play and explore numbers.

The grammar of morality is experience. We don't apprehend morality through a set of instructions, but through internal references to what is right and wrong. In so far as we have been treated with respect, have been heard, valued and recognised, our sense of what is right and what is wrong will reflect that respect. In so far as we have been disrespected, devalued and ignored, our sense of what is right and what is wrong will reflect that disrespect.

We can't learn about right and wrong in any objective sense, for such ideas are always contextual, always relational. Morals are about beliefs, wishes, relative values. In order to create a shared morality we need to do away with the 'shoulds' that usually motivate what we call moral. We need to understand why we believe what we believe and what interferes with our putting into practice what we feel to be the expression of a value system that is harmonious.

From the psychotherapist's perspective, morals are as much the product of unconscious thought as they are of conscious thought. The attack on social morals, exemplified by individual and group acts of destructiveness, will not change as a result of the application of a lesson or two on morality. Acts of rebellion, destruction, deceit and corruption have deep significance for

15

those who engage in them. For some, a perceived wrong is being righted; for others, detachment from meaningful personal relationships produces rage and alienation; while for others, feelings of desperation, of exclusion from the local community or the wider society are so grievously experienced that the only way to express any sense of agency is to show through rejection the felt poverty of the moral code.

We may condemn sexual assault without understanding what has led someone to seek this action. We may condemn violence without understanding that internal tensions could no longer be contained within the individual.

As the fragmentation of our society becomes more obvious and the suffering pierces the boundaries of acceptable behaviour, we may resort to cheap moralising as an attempt to reunite. But such a response is hardly a solution. We need to be braver, to take on board what troubles us about the society we have created. We need to rethink it, to confront the pain, the despair, the exclusion felt by so many, rather than attempt to patch it back together with moralistic bandages.

The Politics of the Spirit:
The Agony of Labour's Defeat

It is easy to underestimate the emotional impact of politics. The process of coming to terms with a fourth consecutive term of Conservative rule and the agony of Labour's defeat may prove to be a long-term process.

We argue passionately about the reasons why we have not been able to replace the government. We try to come to terms with the relative weakness of the opposition and the relative strength of the government. We wonder about the influence of the press, of the media's capacity to turn our minds away from policies, of the creating of bogeymen out of political leaders (let's just watch what is done to prominent politicians over the next few months).

We wonder whether Labour's move to the right has lost it its constituency. We wonder whether Thatcher's dismembering of the Metropolitan authorities and the limits imposed on borough councils have meant that Labour has had no visible voice and no obvious power base. We wonder whether Labour's failure to pick up on and offer leadership on a green agenda, on electoral reform, on women, on issues of class (yes class is alive and well in Britain today – more so than at any time in the last thirty years) and on multi-culturalism, has meant that the important issues raised over the last several decades have been marginalised as much by the opposition as by the government. As we wonder and debate, we may notice we feel angry, wounded, depressed, frustrated and despairing about our capacity to create a new political agenda.

These feelings are an understandable response to the circumstances facing us, but often the emotional responses we have are written out of a political understanding, as though they aren't entirely valid, as though feelings generated by politics are not really that important. But such feelings *are* important. We need to recognise them, to articulate them, to allow them.

Many political activists threw themselves into the election of a new leader of the Labour Party. This provided them with a seemingly important and significant activity as well as a new election to win. But perhaps we should pause here for a moment and ask whether this is indeed such a meaningful activity for all of us. We might ask: what energy is being harnessed in this fight? Where has this energy come from?

It looks to many as though a simple transfer has occurred. The momentum necessarily built up for a general election was transferred to an inter-party one. The considerable feelings of loss, hopelessness, rage and upset caused by the victory of the Conservatives were buried in the need and wish to win which propelled the election campaign. But the understandable wish to win (something, anything!) transferred to the leadership election had the impact of both denying the loss and further disenfranchising all those not deeply involved in the internal politics of the Labour Party. It took up the public space which should have been occupied with political discussion, and pushed it further down the road of a politics of personality and presidentialism.

How might we explain the ridicule and disrespect that greeted Ken Livingstone's and Bernie Grant's candidature? How is it that one of the few Labour Party politicians who has actually run a government (a government so successful it had to be legislated out) could be so summarily dismissed? Could it be that their campaign couldn't be taken seriously because it distracted attention from winning something in the short term? Could it be that a campaign intent upon opening up a conversation – a full discussion about why Labour lost the last election and what different ways of thinking and organising would be required to win the next one – was just too threatening? This campaign's political agenda had an implicit emotional agenda. By questioning the 'safe' agenda in which Labour had lived for the last five years it had the potential to engage with the fear and loss engendered by losing the election rather than covering it up. Whatever the political outcome might have been the broader emotional space would have broadened the scope of our politics and our political responses. But where a politics of fear, where a politics of unmetabolised loss rules, then an agenda of denial and cover-up is required. Any alternative is simply too threatening.

The impact of a fourth Conservative term and the loss of the possibility of a new government has important political and emotional components that have to be assimilated. There are feelings of hopelessness which should not be negated. There are feelings of despair, of fury, of outrage and anxiety which lead to the experience of disenfranchisement, of being disregarded and ignored. Through allowing such feelings we realise how much hope we had riding on a change of government and how much fear and panic there is now that this has not been achieved. Unless we take these feelings on board we will experience greater disaffection, more alienation. Our undigested hopelessness will incline us to disengagement and we will leave politics to the politicians.

People feel bereaved, they feel angry and they feel excluded. Exclusion happens on many levels. Those sections of society who have not been represented since 1979 when Labour was last in power continue to be unrepresented. The poor and the unemployed remain without a voice. Disaffected youth who have been shut out of the system will never find a way in or be listened to. Racism will be sanctioned and will increase rather than being recognised, engaged with and contested, and our society will become even more polarised.

The emotional effects of public policy mean that the quality of *all* our lives is diminished. When the public sphere marginalises so many, the well-being of the culture and of the individual within it is compromised. Politics affects us all in the deepest parts of ourselves and when we live in a society that is so excluding, we are impoverished.

None of this is to say that a hung parliament or a Labour government would have been a solution to the troubles that beset us as a culture. But the hope and the capacity for renewal that such a change would have unleashed, the energy for innovation, for bringing into the public arena a generation excluded from public service, the impetus that would have been felt in the environmental movements, by women, by sections of society who have felt and been excluded, is enormous. Part of the bereavement, the pain, the anger and the loss that so many many people are experiencing is the recognition of the weight of hope – hope of inclusion, hope of change – that was riding on a change of government.

With that hope and loss acknowledged we might begin to create forms that make change possible and exclusion impossible; to find creative expression for our desire to have ourselves represented.

We need to mourn and to grieve. We need to feel our anger and we need to feel our despair. We need to feel all our feelings so that we don't fall into the cynicism which, coupled with hopelessness, fuels the depoliticisation of a culture. Unrecognised feelings in any area shape our responses and reduce our capacity to think clearly and effectively. This is as true of politics as it is of any domestic relations. If we don't allow our feelings a chance to be aired then we will use argument and ideology to constrain them, to bind them up, and our politics – far from being guided by principle – will incorporate a great sense of fear.

Homophobia: The Hate Afraid to Speak Its Name

The alleged discovery of a gene for homosexuality has been greeted variously as: 'It's not our/their fault'; 'This is as biologically determined as heterosexuality', and 'This gene fault can be remedied.'

Although there is considerable relief in sections of the gay community, who claim that this study can be read as a legitimation of homosexuality and that it represents a move away from regarding homosexuality as a perverse practice to acknowledging it as a natural state, the study – like much of the work on heritability of IQ, social attitudes and so on – is hardly convincing. Nevertheless, it allows us to address culturally rife homophobic attitudes.

Alongside the assault on single mothers where women in vastly different categories are lumped together to serve an ideological purpose not of their making, homosexuals have also been seen as a monolithic, unidimensional group and they are routinely charged with undermining the moral fabric of the community and the family. Even while we recognise that these charges are nonsense, the habitual homophobia we encounter around us at every turn creates and reinforces the notion that different (i.e. non-heterosexual) sexual practices are wrong.

Psychoanalysis is, in part, an account of human sexual development. Part of Freud's project was to explain how, as he put it, the polymorphously perverse infant enters human culture through the categories of masculinity and femininity. Heterosexuality is hardly a necessary outcome. Erotic object choice – whether we find the same sex or the opposite sex sexually attractive, or both, – is fluid up to a point in time at which it becomes, for most people, fixed.

The current debate about the origins of male homosexuality raises many important questions, but what it rarely focuses on is the fear and panic that motivates so much homophobia. Why are we as a culture so deeply afraid of same-sex erotic love? Why do male–male love relationships and female–female relationships so alarm us? What is being touched in people so that they find a response of rejection, of disgust, even of violent hate, welling up in them? Even among those who consider themselves enlightened, and even among some homosexuals, a set of internalised negative attitudes exists. If we examine some of those unwittingly held prejudices we can engage more profoundly with what disturbs us about different sexualities.

Sexuality is partly a choice about the nature of attachment. Sexual intimacy, the exchange of pleasure between bodies, carries a deep significance. For many practising heterosexuals, sexuality already encodes within it the emotional tracings of earlier intimacy with the same-sex parent or peer. For girls especially, their first love relationship, their first sensual relationship, the relationship which first embraced them physically and psychically, was most likely to have been with a woman – with mother.

Although we would not characterise the mother–daughter relationship as a homosexual attachment, the profound significance of that first love lives in all daughters' psyches at some level. Indeed in the passage to heterosexuality, it is not so much that girls give up their love for their mothers; rather, that relationship becomes a model for other relationships, and subsequent intimacies are built on top of that primary relationship.

Many women discover that their intimate relations with men embody aspects of their relationship with their mothers. Even at the sexual level many women report that it is the combination of a kind of maternal cuddling and hugging from their partners and a more passionate erotic exchange that is meaningful for them. In other words, within heterosexuality, for women, is the memory and continued longing for sensual acceptance and embracing from a woman.

The fact that our culture makes this exchange between most adult women so impermissible that it can't be recognised or explored results in a kind of compulsive heterosexuality being sought and adhered to, making heterosexuality a rather falser or more defensive position than need be. If we could accept that for women heterosexuality includes within it an aspect of homosexuality, we could allow that awareness to lessen the need to repudiate, to hate or fear our own female homosexuality and thus homosexuals as a group.

Female negative responses to male homosexuality often reflect a feeling of rejection. The woman experiences a man's choice of a male love object as a negation of her and her femininity. This painful experience of rejection then becomes transposed into a defence – becoming rejecting oneself. The lack of sexual recognition that a woman may unconsciously rely on to locate herself leaves her feeling stranded; and out of that combination of feelings – rejection and loss – comes the motivation to criticise and reject homosexual practice. The taking on and mimicry of aspects of femininity by gay men can upset many heterosexual women. Behind the upset is a feeling of invasion as though women are losing an aspect of their private culture. More accurately, the mimicry represents a threat to our rigidly divided sex roles, and if it can be understood in this way rather than as a predatory act, women may be able to find its implicit critique releasing rather than threatening.

For many heterosexually inclined men, the fear that motivates much homophobia contains within it both the wish to engage in homosexual relations (recent research estimates that between

40 per cent and 70 per cent of heterosexually defined men have had or have sexual relations with other men) and the fear of it. Part of what fuels the expressed rejection is the perception that it is possible for men to relate to one another in ways that are less competitive, less adversarial, less about positioning than conventional male bonding. This is not to say that homosexual relations are necessarily less hierarchical, but they do implicitly contain a critique of orthodox gender roles in which men's desires to find more complex ways of relating to each other is often thwarted.

Many men feel devoid of emotionally rich friendships. They fail to disclose their feelings to one another, concentrating instead on external interests they can share. The longing to disclose and the difficulty or fear of doing so are bypassed by being unconsciously projected on to male homosexuals, who then are seen to have this ability. Homosexuals are turned into 'other', seen as different and hence threatening.

Beneath much of homophobia are individuals' desires to connect with their own gender in ways that are circumscribed by many cultural practices. The taboo on homosexuality has been internalised by us all to some extent or another, and while this gene research may be of little scientific significance in the long run, its prominence at this time gives us a chance to think through and out of some of our reflexive homophobic responses.

Tabloid Treatment: Politics and David Mellor

Many commentators, including the writer of the *Guardian* leader, noted the way the Conservative Heritage Minister David Mellor's resignation displaced coverage of the recall of parliament. What wasn't discussed was the psychological implications for all of us of Mellor's resignation and the psychological impact of having the economic crisis wiped off our front pages.

No one disputes that this was a tabloid-forced resignation. It is well known that tabloid editors are sitting on some pretty juicy photos of other very senior parliamentarians in compromising positions. So we can reasonably judge that the choice to go after Mellor had important political meaning in terms of who he was and what he represented. At the same time it was a convenient running scandal that could be used to propitious effect.

Sections of the tabloid press had something serious to gain if David Mellor could be dislodged from his position. With the departure of the defender of the BBC, tabloid owners were jumping up and down for joy savouring the thought of increased profits as they extend their influence into tabloid television.

But their victory has an additional significance at a psychological level. It gave them a chance to extend what has become their empire of amnesia to the airwaves. The diet of so-called news and pap that fills their pages contributes to a cultural malaise, a profound disaffection, a disenfranchisement from the body politic which is then consolidated by more fluff. In this period of enormous distress on the economic and social front, we desperately need real engagement with the issues of the day. Neither the tabloids nor the so-called qualities meet their obligations to us here.

This is why the timing of the resignation is significant. For on the evening when the government and the opposition parties were debating the fiscal débâcle of the decade, both newspapers and TV, with the solitary exception of Channel 4 news, led with the titillating story of the Mellor resignation.

What are the psychological costs of reporting events in this way? What does it mean psychologically that the first parliamentary discussion following devaluation – a discussion which contested the Tory claim that they knew what they were up to – was upstaged instead of occupying centre stage in the public domain? Can we not argue that the result of transferring attention from the political nature of both these events into a superficial account of Labour leader John Smith's personal performance and David Mellor's personal tragedy (or well-deserved fall from grace, depending on your point of view) is an expression of how depoliticised we are now becoming as a culture?

If we say yes, that we are indeed being pushed to distance ourselves, dissociate ourselves, devolve political responsibilities to small, unaccountable groups, then enormous psychological costs ensue.

When we invest our confidence in others and are then let down it has debilitating effects. If we are betrayed by those whom we trust, we are shattered. Betrayal of the citizen, of the responsibilities of public office, engenders feelings of rage, dissociation and inauthenticity. When, aided and abetted by the way the news is reported, our political leadership exhibits callous disregard for the public, and when the betrayal cannot be spoken of or assigned responsibility, we have to find a way to cope somehow. We may try against all odds to preserve our limited political relationships because that is all we perceive can exist. We soothe our knowledge of what is going on with palliatives of one kind or another to cover the pain we feel, and recast as acceptable what has betrayed us.

The betrayal many have experienced over the highly visible and yet denied economic collapse of Britain and the refusal of political leadership to admit to that reality, causes a population deep confusion. If we look to the press and TV for dialogue between leader and led, betrayer and betrayed, we see that instead of genuine discourse we are offered trivia and distraction.

When people find no recognition of their perception of a situation, when personal responses instead of being acknowledged or mirrored are distorted, they face the difficult psychological task of bearing that perception alone. As the distance between what one observes and what one is told grows, the isolated individual feels invalidated and responds perhaps by becoming angry, paranoid (conspiracy theories) or withdrawn.

While part of one's psychic energy may continue to be available for political interaction, and indeed still wants it, another part may become overwhelmed by feelings of despair and distress. This part transfers energy from political relationships to personality politics in the psyche's attempt to protect personal integrity by focusing on less threatening issues.

But the withdrawal involves a withdrawal from an actual relationship. That disappointing relationship is then not simply rejected: it is simultaneously absorbed as the measure, as a standard, of the kinds of political relationship that are possible. When we discover that what we see, what we judge to be important, is ignored, we are negated. We may rebel and rage or we may become cynical. If we fail to hook up with others with whom we can confirm our perceptions, if we are allowed no forum in which to speak or be heard, we risk de-empower-ment and infantilisation. We will be tempted to withdraw and be swamped by hopeless feelings about our relationship to the body politic. This, I fear, is what we face as a culture in Britain today.

This annihilation of our desire and will to participate is at the heart of the effect of tabloid newspapers and tabloid television. If our public organs render our voices inaudible, if our oppo-sition, our questions and our authentic engagement can be curtailed, then a vacuum is created into which a diet of inconse-quential musings and pseudo-importances is dumped. We will learn about the details of one man's sexual proclivities, we will be fed an analysis of personalities as a substitute for a vital relationship with the public culture.

As the unofficial handmaiden to current ideology, tabloid journalism works with those who find thinking and questioning in public inconvenient. With its addictive pap it is the antithesis of thinking and questioning. No wonder its pages become the vehicle for the present reactionary cant on education. Real learning, and our healthy preoccupation with and delight in it, is the absolute opposite of the deadening preoccupations we are offered by tabloid journalism. Real learning is an affirmation of life and personal agency. It builds up our curiosity and leads us to unpredictable and exciting places. An engaged and alive populace would leave tabloid journalism out in the cold just as it would refuse the present limited relationship with power that our government offers us.

The Victim Inside the Bully

In a moving moment from Andy Metcalf's BBC TV film *Dot, Top Men and the Joeys*, two men in prison embrace in recognition of their vulnerability. One of the men, unable to cope with the bullying he has experienced in the post-penal hostel where he has been a resident, gets himself in trouble and finds himself back in prison where a highly elaborated system of bullying, of relations of dominance, prevails.

This Everyman film explores the relationship between bullying and vulnerability and the attempt of the hostel warden, Dot, to contain the bullying by helping those picked on – the vulnerables, as she calls them – find a way to stand up for themselves. What Dot realises and hopes to convey to the men is that vulnerability and bullying are two sides of a coin.

Bullying is a phenomenon entwined in our social practices, confronting us in many aspects of daily life and causing great distress and destruction. Bullying between children in schools is now understood to be a very serious problem, in some cases leading to attempted suicide. On the job, the bullying manager or colleague reduces productivity and infuses the workplace with a menacing atmosphere. In the home, the bullying spouse

29

frightens his or her partner into compliance. Many of our institutions – from the fagging system of the public school to the promotion of bullies in the prison system – embody and depend upon relations of dominance and submission.

While today's representation of these institutional systems of domination is cloaked in the language of leadership and of learning responsibility, in many of their fundamental aspects these systems depend on terror, intimidation and violence for ordering relations between people. In the less crude systems, such as those in training institutions, the Civil Service, old-style corporations and political and religious sects, authority and loyalty are enforced through exclusion, secrecy and hierarchy. One becomes initiated into a hierarchical system which exaggerates and exploits power differentials. One learns to mimic the behaviour of the emulated by adopting their practices towards one's juniors. By biding time until one accrues institutional power, one pledges a form of allegiance to the institution and its hierarchy.

Bullying is an exercise of terror: it externalises and foists on to another, or others, the out-of-control feelings that create internal pressure and sense of powerlessness. These feelings become translated into acts of domination. The impetus to bully, the motivation to bully is gathered together out of a set of excruciatingly insecure feelings so hard to tolerate that they seek a form of relief in acts of aggressive intimidation.

The person led to bullying by his or her explosive inner state reproduces a form of expression already known to him or her. The bully is most likely to be someone who has been more than a one-time victim of bullying, or who has been a witness to repetitive bullying. The horror of repeated experiences of being tyrannised has produced feelings of 'being out of control' and belittled. At the same time, in order to cope with being aggressed upon the 'victim' identifies with the assailant as a way of surviving the encounter. The victim enters into both experiences as a means of escaping the horror of victimisation.

The capacity of the hurt and attacked person to split into (at least) two parts – one which identifies with the bully and one which retains the knowledge of the bludgeoning experience – helps us understand why bullies tend to pick on those they perceive as vulnerable or whom they can render vulnerable. In taking on the persona and action of the aggressor, they crush the part of themselves that has been desperately hurt, dismembered and overpowered. They reassure themselves that they have the capacity to withstand hurt. By inflicting it on others and remaining unmoved, they survive their most dreaded experiences. Bullying reassures them that they are invincible, that the shame, humiliation and hurt of psychic dismemberment can be withstood.

At an interpersonal level bullying can be understood in several ways. It is most clearly a mechanism for dumping distress. And as we have seen it is an exercise of coercion which demands a response of compliance. The compliance it elicits ensures that the bullying will continue. For if bullying is about the fear of facing hurt, vulnerability and anger being converted into aggression, then those who submit to bullying confirm in the mind of the bully that vulnerability, hurt and anger are appropriately dealt with in this manner. Bullying becomes a compulsive act, allowing the bully to escape their problems by conferring them on another. But because the underlying causes of the bullying have not been assimilated the act of aggression must repeatedly be played out.

Beyond these meanings, bullying is also a search for containment and the pursuit of an encounter which will offer a boundary that resists and refuses the intimidation. The bully seeks a response of imperviousness, through which border his or her problem cannot seep but will be addressed. If a barrier were held and not breached, if the recipient of the bullying were to refuse to be cowed, the bully could have a shot at re-encountering the distress he or she is continually trying to unload.

This barrier, this ability to find the strength to resist menace, is what the hostel warden Dot means when she talks about finding a way to stand up for yourself. This capacity not only allows the victim to reject the conditions of victimisation, it confronts the bully with a limit. The struggle then moves from the confines of becoming the bully or the bullied to learning how to tolerate and then be finished with the pain that has led to the situation.

Emotional Responsibility

Over the last decade, we as a culture and as individuals have become more aware of the impact of emotional abuse on all of us. As a result we have been forced to try to begin to face our fear and our ignorance of emotional processes.

We are surrounded by alarming statistics about the level of personal distress. According to the Mental Health Foundation, one in four people in Britain (i.e. 12 million adults) suffers 'mental illness' at some time. Thousands upon thousands of people seek to soothe their suffering through drinking, developing eating problems, or taking psychotropic drugs. And terrifyingly high rates of sexual abuse, random violence and destruction impel us to recognise that there is something quite amiss in the way we treat each other.

Many people continue to write off the evidence about the impact of early relationships on a person's experience of him or herself and what they then feel able to do with their lives. But there is wider acceptance of the considerable damage to personal esteem that results from consistent emotional damage. The links

This is an edited version of a talk for NewPin.

between how we are treated, how we regard ourselves and how we relate to others are now very well established. Few doubt that children who are treated with respect, who are enjoyed and loved, listened to and responded to, will grow up feeling easy in relationships, will approach their wider environment with confidence and will in turn be interested and engaged with their children, peers, co-workers and so on.

Experiences of appropriate attention beget self-esteem. A person who has been part of positive experiences from early on feels confident and whole. They feel, hurt, cry, grieve, rant, enjoy, laugh, suffer and play. These emotional capacities are available to them in an undistorted form. Good feelings don't need to be forced into hiding or displayed inappropriately; sad feelings are acknowledged and lived through. Conflict presents as difficulty rather than being turned into anxiety, while need and desire are felt as legitimate self-expression. Such a person takes their wholeness and the range of emotional responses available to them for granted. Connected to themselves in this way, they are able to give spontaneously, to set boundaries and receive.

But for many many people, this scenario of well-being seems unattainable. Their emotional lives are rent with hurt. They feel depleted, misunderstood, incapable of responding out of generosity, befuddled by anxiety. They may find that their emotional repertoire is limited to a few tracks: anger or joy, guilt or fear, depression or confusion. They may create dramas around them to express their hurt and confusions, and almost any trigger can become the mechanism by which they try to bring forward the injustices they feel, the anger they want recognised, the hurt that wants soothing, the conflict acknowledged. In creating a drama, they attempt to divest themselves of the hurt, to finally be done with the feeling, but, unable to express themselves outside of the drama, they remain misunderstood and isolated.

Hemmed in by limiting emotional responses which reiterate patterns of undigested meaning they are driven to dump those feelings out. This need to evacuate becomes paramount because transformation of the feelings is elusive. As one empties out one's bad feelings on another, one participates in and perpetuates the cycle of emotional abuse. Emotional damage contaminates the interpersonal sphere, and if the recipient of the bad feelings has no way to understand their origin, they will hold them until they too can pass them on.

So emotional damage is a component of emotional abuse. When individuals, families and groups of people are emotionally damaged they can't help hurting themselves or those around them. In trying to rid themselves of their own pain they unwittingly damage others. Unable to face, contain and digest their personal pain they must fling it out into their local emotional environment where it is picked up by others.

Babies often appear to be in great distress. On the face of it they seem inconsolable and they can create great tension and anxiety around them when they cry and scream. If the caregiver is alarmed by the distress, and responds by getting anxious or by feeling compelled to silence the baby, the baby learns that its emissions, its self, are somehow not all right. It may protest and whimper but eventually it will find a way to concede on the surface and to present an acceptable self to its caregiver – a self that can be received. But it will live with a deep sense of alienation and a sense that who it is is somehow fundamentally wrong.

But a caregiver who has the ability to tolerate a baby's stress, to receive it without being frightened of it, to accept it as valid and at the same time render it back to the baby as manageable and understandable, makes it possible for the baby to settle. The baby then feels that its upset has been responded to, has been returned in a less frightening form. It can have feelings without overwhelming another or being overwhelmed itself.

This communication between caregiver and baby, which is a vital component in the building of self-esteem, of feeling legitimate and all right inside oneself, is an important model for interpersonal communication. But as a culture we are often deficient in tolerating and helping another to reframe or reshape their feelings.

While I am not advocating that we treat one another as infants, I am asking us to look at a key aspect of the baby–caregiver interaction. The process by which the baby's feelings are received and responded to could be an important model for relating to both our own and each other's emotional productions. At present we are often so frightened by others' emotions that we attempt to shield ourselves from them; meanwhile we may not be able to take responsibility for our own.

Being emotionally responsible has two different parts to it; articulating and listening. We need to develop the skills of talking, of finding the language that can express our emotional states, to specify how and what we feel even if we don't yet understand why. And we need to clear the space to listen to another, to resist the push to silence or to dissuade another out of their feelings or to argue when their emotional experience diverges from ours or threatens our perspective.

As we can begin to take responsibility for decoding and then admitting to our own feelings we may be less impelled to repress them or to use them as an assault on others. We may build up the confidence to articulate them, to act on them rather than act them out. If we can answer how we feel, if we can begin to listen when asking how another is, we can set in train the possibility of containing and engaging with our and others' emotional responses.

Emotional Havoc

In discussing emotional responsibility I suggested that when a person has difficulty in accepting his or her emotional experience, that experience can spill over and disrupt the emotional field of others. It then bounces back in a distorted form, causing interpersonal confusion and misunderstanding.

When we encounter problematic feelings we either repress, digest or displace them. At different times our psyche uses all three strategies. Some of us can handle a wide range of feelings but, more commonly, there are areas of emotional life that prove difficult for each of us.

Danielle is extremely panicked by death; Joan by feelings of helplessness. John can't tolerate feeling dependent and Len is scared by the tears of others. Such responses are by no means uncommon. What causes the difficulty is when those who are sensitive in one way or another are unaware of their reactions. Before they can find a way to tolerate a particularly troublesome feeling, they sever themselves from it, creating a certain amount of emotional havoc in their local environment.

For example a child feels sad. His father feels discomfort that his child is hurting. Uneasy with coping with sadness inside himself, he tries to jolly the child along; the child then gets out of control, tearful and whiny. This enrages the father, who snarls: 'I'll give you something to really cry about.' A fight ensues in which the child's original pain is diverted and in which the father ends up feeling both useless himself and annoyed with his child for being weak. His own difficulty with sadness remains unrecognised.

The process of projection involves the attempt to rid oneself of an indigestible feeling through separating oneself from it. We may then more safely recognise, criticise and or respond to what we perceive to be the difficult feeling in another. Danielle is panicked by death. John can't tolerate feeling dependent. But projection also allows one to get close to the disavowed feeling by embracing that very same feeling in another. So Danielle is able to comfort others and in fact is a bereavement counsellor, while John is very good at finding emotional waifs to care for, and so on.

The mechanisms associated with projection enable us to experience our own disturbing feelings vicariously, to connect to one another, to imagine what another is feeling, to become emotionally attuned and, as I suggested in 'Emotional Responsibility', they enable adults to interpret babies' emotional utterances.

Projection then is part of ordinary emotional exchange, but if it is the main device the psyche employs – that is, if emotional experience has to be continually gutted and dumped out – then the individual is left empty of feeling and continually has to engage with her or his feelings second-hand as a way to fill the void and reconnect with the displaced feelings.

These dynamics happen in all relationships. Those between couples, if not sorted out, contribute to the daily aggro and undermining that makes intimate relationships less easygoing than both parties would wish them to be. Jean and Laurie were deciding on a holiday for several months hence. Jean favoured the beach and Laurie the mountains. Jean's passionately expressed need to hang out in sand and sun was at first resentfully received by Laurie, but in time Laurie reluctantly deferred and agreed to a beach holiday. Although Jean was thrilled, she hid her pleasure from Laurie. She felt guilty and surprised that her desire had been met. By hiding her excitement, she failed to acknowledge that Laurie, albeit reluctantly, had given in to her. It was as though neither of them was getting what she wanted. For Laurie the act of giving had been submerged under a resentment that concealed the act of giving.

The disavowed feelings which threatened to ruin the holiday for both ran thus. Jean was uncomfortable with conflict. She was also extremely uneasy with the notion of winning, so when Laurie agreed to the beach holiday her difficulty with winning and her difficulty with handling conflict were joined.

These feelings were to an extent disowned and thrown into the space between Laurie and her. For Laurie's part, the wish to be flexible jarred with an inflexible tendency. In opting for the beach, she was trying to engage with her rigidity and she felt that the very act of giving absolved her of the need to take responsibility for her comments about luscious mountains. She failed to see these as antagonistic and as antithetical to her giving. She too disliked conflict and perceived Jean as being ungrateful and only too willing to start a fight.

The shared difficulty with conflict, Jean's trouble with receiving and Laurie's with bending, sat like a mess of tangled necklaces in the relationship space. As one tried to unpick the knot in one direction so the tangle looked like unravelling, but the pressure increased elsewhere, threatening to break the fragile connections.

The projected feelings needed to be reclaimed so that a circle could, as it were, be drawn around each person's emotional experience demarcating their individual feelings rather than each one hoping that if they displaced the feelings they could be handled by the other. The circle would allow Laurie to experience her act of giving while accepting the loss of the mountain holiday. Her inability to handle her own decision within *her* emotional sphere took away from her experience of giving. Her giving became tinged with resentment and she felt bad on two accounts: not having the holiday she would have preferred, and being so ungracious about it.

Jean meanwhile needed to pull back into her emotional sphere the fact of getting the holiday that suited her. She needed not to conceal her pleasure but to be open about it and to acknowledge Laurie's 'sacrifice' of her wish for a mountain holiday.

Although this is a very simple and common example which the reader may feel is almost too trivial to follow, it is worth considering because it encapsulates the kinds of transaction in which displaced emotional responses infect the interpersonal field and turn the initial gestures – of saying what one wants, of giving – into antagonistic positions.

The effort to own one's own emotional responses before they commingle with a partner's; to recognise a personal internal conflict rather than project it is difficult but it is enormously valuable. Taking personal emotional responsibility means less contamination and misunderstanding. It means one has the emotional space to approach personal difficulties rather than seeking relief and failing to find it through displacement.

Secrets

We all have secrets.
        Beginning in childhood we bury painful, forbidden unfathomable experiences deep within us where they fester in silence. We have our secret ambitions; our secret longings; our secret wishes and our secret worries. Fearing ridicule or disdain, we hide our feelings from others and eventually from ourselves. We have secrets of the soul, secrets of the heart and secrets of the conscience.

In our waking life, the festering material of our secret selves makes us miss a beat in conversation as our unconscious steers us away from areas too sensitive to touch. At night, our dreams create incomprehensible images, further concealing in riddles and symbolism the secrets we are trying to keep from ourselves.

Understanding secrets is a part of our development. From childhood onwards we know ourselves and the world, as the hazy secrets we couldn't comprehend, slowly, one by one, begin to make sense. Curiosity about life leads us to want to uncover secrets, to understand how the disconnected pieces fit together. As adults we need to understand the emotional secrets of our childhood, to comprehend the terror we felt when we saw our father weeping, when we heard our parents whispering, when we received seemingly arbitrary decisions and orders. We need to understand why we couldn't know why. To understand why we couldn't ask.

Secrets are part of the fabric of relationships. Secrets both characterise and cement closeness. Girls exchange secrets with one another and promise fealty through the holding of these secrets. Women friends keep each other's secrets: secrets of infidelity, of private unhappiness, of longings that daren't be spoken too loud.

Men pledge themselves to one another to hold the secrets of war; of the club; of the workplace. They keep the secrets of the nation, of male bonding, of patriarchy.

Lovers create a secret world together – a cocoon where their raptures can be protected. The secrecy of the love affair, the details that can only be experienced and felt together enhance the passion, the love, the desire.

And in families, how many are held together by the family secret – skeletons in the cupboard which bind together unhappily related individuals as strongly as superglue?

What we observe and learn in the family is a model for the wider world. We see that secrets are everywhere. There are secrets that mustn't be spoken of at home. There are secrets that mustn't be spoken of at school. There are secrets that mustn't be spoken of at work. There are secrets that mustn't be spoken of in wartime. There are secrets that mustn't be spoken of in peace.

In politics, in the Civil Service, in local government and in the police, secrecy is the name of the game. All societies have secrets. In Germany, 'Die Generation Danach' (The generation after Hitler) has still to confront its parents while North American citizens are kept in the dark about the true cost in lives of the war in the Gulf. But in Britain we are particularly addicted to secrecy. In the public sphere we live with the most comprehensive Official Secrets Act while our personal relationships are all too often characterised by the lowered voice and the averted gaze. Secrets suffuse our public and our private relationships and in so doing compromise our relationship to self.

Secrets permeate all our relations. Secrecy is a national sport. Two-facedness is so common a practice that visitors from other cultures intending to stay here need to be inducted into the delicate process of reading the covert signals of real intentions. While we think of our facility with secrets as protective, even deliciously enjoyable, they are often a cheap and sham intimacy. Secrets can have a destructive and divisive function. Where on the surface they may offer a shared intimacy and closeness, they also engender suspicion and a fear of difference. Where they appear to protect us they may also create havoc and hurt. Where they are perpetrated publicly they breed contempt and distrust in a spurned citizenry.

The underbelly of the secret, that is to say its negative functions, is worth exploring. Why do we need secrets? Why are secrets so alluring? What would we be doing with the information if it wasn't secret?

In politics those answers are all too obvious. We would be informed; we could act with knowledge; we could be a literate and empowered citizenry grappling with difficult decisions, struggling with policy: in short, creating our world. But schooled in a culture of secrecy we are forced to dabble instead in the sport of finding out; of learning how to disregard disinformation rather than learning to exercise power.

In personal and social life, secrets have equally disastrous results. We conceal homosexuality in the family in order to protect our homosexual child or niece. But this attempt at protective behaviour in a homophobic society is construed as an act of shame. The secret becomes an act which makes our child, our niece, an unintended pariah.

What we dislike or find hard to understand in ourselves we try to disown. What we fear or what we envy in others we make less fearful (at least in the short term) by transferring it on to another whom we then differentiate ourselves from: 'We're not like them. We're better, different, special.' Through the mechanism of projection our disowned attributes end up adhered to others. We defend our sense of ourselves by avoiding being sullied by 'Them'.

Secrets come in many forms but we can break them down into two main categories. There are secrets which engender shame and can only be shared in situations of trust. In this category we might include secrets about sexual abuse; about a partner's infidelity; about a painful memory of meanness perpetrated against another.

The psychological function of sharing such a secret is to build a bridge to intimacy. One exposes one's vulnerabilities, hurts and shame to another and one hopes not to be rejected. The acceptance one is offered is internalised and helps dissolve some of the shame and hurt. The sharing of a secret in this context is more than simply relieving or unburdening oneself. The sharing allows the pain to heal and allows whatever was stunted – a feeling, an activity, a guiltily held desire – to regrow. It is liberating and cleansing.

The other category of secrets is about exclusion. These secrets are attempts to create a conspiratorial world in which its members can feel affirmed. Into this category we might most obviously put political secrets, power cliques at work, within clubs and so on. The psychological function of the conspiratorial secret is essentially defensive. Group A is not to know what group B is doing. Group B wants the privileges it has to be protected, to be beyond the knowledge of the other, be that a group, a class, a race, a religion, a nationality, a sexuality or a gender. The conspiratorial kind of secret, rather than liberating people, coercively ties them together. One can be suffocated by the secrets of one's religion; by sexual or social norms that must be upheld without being spoken of. The holders of the secrets are not asked to share, treasure and to help the other free themselves of some shame, or act on a hidden desire, as in the first category of secret. The holders are asked rather to collude in inequity; to enter a situation which will create or preserve a difference, to secure an advantage.

Secrets are not the same as privacy, and they are not the same as discretion. We all have the need to be discreet, and we all have the need to be private. We need to hold things inside ourselves: ideas and feelings that make up our sense of the unique, the personal, the me-ness of self. Privacy is about self-respect, about self-knowledge and self-consciousness. It is only possible to really share with another if one has a sense of a private, contained self. A self that can surprise and nourish.

By contrast, secrets of exclusion, conspiratorial secrets, are about limiting, about hiding, about disowning and fear. When we engage in making a secret bond, we can help ourselves by asking: who is it for, what is its function, who is it hurting, what would happen if we refused to enter into the intrigue? And perhaps above all what we need to confront is what might happen if we were to resist its pull.

Peace in the Middle East

The historic agreement reached between the Israeli government and the Palestinian Liberation Organisation (compared in significance to the collapse of the Berlin Wall) gives rise
to both hope and fear. While much attention has rightly been
focused on the fairness/unfairness of the deal and the economic
and social tasks facing both peoples, the dimension that is rarely
addressed is the psychological work necessary to change a
situation from one of hate and fight into one in which people
with antagonistic interests find ways of living together.

Over the last few years we have seen the enormous difficulties
that have ensued from the political unification of Germany. The
fantasy of harmonious integration has been short-lived. The
substantial problems involved in the bringing together of that
divided society requires examination of the mechanisms of
prejudice and fear. But the politicians – having opportunistically
exploited the receptivity of both societies for union – have to a
large extent allowed the hard work of unification to be subsumed under a wave of intolerance.

Before the demise of the Berlin Wall, the leadership of both
societies sought relief from their internal problems by renaming

them in terms of their relation to each other so that the East's problem was the existence of the West, and vice versa. The economic, social and psychological problems of East and West Germany before 1989 found a plausible, emotionally resonant explanation in the view that the other was culpable. Both peoples, both states were still dealing with the legacy of smashed imperial ambition. The East included a similar number of Fascists to the West. The transformation of Fascist ideology into state communist and western capitalism respectively bypassed the essential mourning, grief, shame and anger that Germany and Germans needed to go through in order to come to terms with their history.

In place of dealing with history we had the erection of an external enemy. Now with the need to integrate the two Germanies we see the deflection of these challenges into racism: foreign workers, first-generation Germans and refugees are targeted and attacked. The substantial economic and social issues facing Germany are diverted. Germans can bond together under the umbrella of either racism or anti-racism. And while we might feel greatly relieved about the anti-racist demonstrations and actions, which are honourable and crucial, and while they do produce the profoundly important experiences of people coming together in solidarity, the fact is that Germany's problems are being conceived of in racial terms rather than as a set of exceptionally difficult social, economic, political and emotional issues to be reworked.

So too in the Middle East. If the agreement being negotiated can be made to stand – and it is a big if, because it seems unbalanced against the Palestinians – both the Israelis and the Palestinians have to learn how to transform themselves.

Both Israelis and Palestinians have, for different reasons, been able to call upon their peoples to hate the others. This hate may seem entirely justified on the part of the Palestinians who lost their homeland. The political problems this loss created are incalculable; the political creativity needed to manage war and the Palestinian diaspora are phenomenal. Despite much imaginative work within the camps, and through PLO cadres, many Palestinians have been pulled into hate and fundamentalism.

The Israelis for their part have surprised sections of liberal world opinion by their treatment of the Palestinians. They have been marked by the pogroms and the Holocaust (and since the fall of the Soviet Union a serious upturn in anti-Semitism), and many have wondered how a people so brutalised and oppressed could create conditions of oppression for others. Israeli Jews disdain the notion that their Holocaust suffering means they should be placed on a different moral plane when it comes to defending their interests. Nevertheless one might ask what psychological mechanisms are at work that make it possible for a diasporadic people to accept their government's visiting a diaspora on another people. Whether or not we judge the original role of the British as more culpable than that of contemporary Israel in terms of the set-up of the Middle East, we have to take into account the diasporic conversion.

Israeli Jews may have been given no place for the guilt they experienced in taking another's homeland. The Zionist ideology which saw Palestine as belonging to the Jews has, in recent times, swept aside recognition of the emotional meaning of dispossessing the Palestinians. It has made moral and historical assertions about biblical rights when what was needed was a chance for Israeli Jews to understand the meaning of displacing others. Jews know a version of this feeling from their own displacement. It is emotionally resonant and can be used to support an ideology, but it is not a political or a psychological solution.

None of this is to say that the main issues in world politics are psychological. Political conflicts are about real antagonistic interests. However, political clarity has to include attending to basic emotional tasks and the emotional fallout from political actions. Otherwise unexamined feelings of fear, despair, hate and cynicism can easily be exploited by less than perfect politicians until the situation implodes.

Fundamentalism is a solution to which people can become

receptive when political complexities appear too great to manage. Fundamentalism represents a form of denial, of splitting. There is an attempt to unite disparate forces by shifting difficulties to outside parties and by rallying to a cause. The complexities of the situation are then seemingly reduced and seemingly manageable. Nations, peoples, groups who have opposing interests create a reason to exist in their rejection of the other. But this is not politics. It is prejudice, fear, and all too often the cowardice of political leaders. It is the fear that governments all over the world exploit. True, there is legitimate hate and fear and cowardice in politics. But often the apparently insoluble (and perhaps really insoluble) internal political problems are manipulated into the image of the other as enemy.

The historic injustices which have come together in the Middle East will continue to produce hatred unless the region's politicians can lead an exploration of the issues rather than hide behind rhetoric. The vital issues of guilt, of living side by side, of dealing with each people's internal problems, of managing the Western influence in predominantly Arab cultures, of the economic tensions and exploitation within and between cultures, of the gender issues, of the legacy of hate on all sides, of the internal issues of racism in Israel will remain unaddressed, ready to incite fundamentalist responses.

The accord is significant in that each side recognises for the first time the legitimacy of the other: the Israelis recognise the PLO, and the PLO the State of Israel. This recognition is a crucial political and psychological step in the making of new meaning and practice in the Middle East. It begins the tortuous but necessary process of healing the divisions of the family within, of recognising differences between the aspirations and histories of different Israeli Jews and the differences and aspirations of the Palestinians. Attention to the *internal* differences, to recognising, accepting and finding a way to work politically on those is crucial if the psychological mechanisms that produce hate and fundamentalism are not to win.

What's Really Going on Here?

*Feelings are not good, bad,
productive or unproductive. They
simply are. Why we feel a
particular way given a particular
set of circumstances is, of course,
analysable. Often we discover that
our initial feeling hides other
feelings that we consider for one
reason or other to be
unmanageable.*

Anger

Crude expositions of psychotherapy would have us believe that expressing one's anger – if not to the person then to a pillow or some such substitute – is of enormous benefit. And of course it may well be. But anger is a complex emotion and just as often defies easy explanation or uniform solutions.

For many, the straightforward expression of anger is untroublesome. They feel angry and can acknowledge that anger without causing unwarranted stress to the recipient of the anger or to themselves. Indeed the expression of the anger is strengthening: it accurately reflects and is a direct response to some infringement. Feeling and showing the anger restores the feeling of agency, and says, in effect: this is unacceptable. I will not be treated in this way.

We are probably all familiar with the argument that – for a variety of reasons to do with upbringing and cultural patterning – women tend to find the recognition of anger in themselves difficult (it gets turned against themselves), while men are more comfortable with this form of emotional expression, relying on it – in many cases rather too readily – to take the weight of other feelings.

In broad strokes these gendered caricatures may be more or less accurate. They reflect, I believe, two poles in relation to this difficult emotion which are worth exploring. One of these poles is a readiness to anger which, of course, can be found in men or women.

There are people who seem to greet the world with anger. They are sensitive to the nuance of injustice in almost any encounter – politics, the behaviour of people who serve them in shops, late trains, foiled plans, personal relationships, and so on. On the face of it, their anger is justifiable. It is outrageous that political deeds can be so destructive. It is annoying to feel one is doing shopkeepers a favour by buying from them. It is inconvenient and frustrating to wait for late trains or to have one's plans changed.

But, we could ask, is instant arousal to anger a helpful response or does the fact that all such events cause one to feel anger hide from view more problematic emotions that are being stirred up? What is the temporary gain of feeling anger, and what are the potential losses? What is the injustice being sniffed out when such people continually experience anger in personal relationships, when they find themselves railing against their spouses, lovers, children, family and friends? When difference or disagreement cannot be tolerated and instead creates a wedge between the self and other?

Such anger, I believe, is not about injustice *per se*, but about one's emotional responses to it. The anger functions as a shield against hurt, disappointment, powerlessness, emotions that in themselves are so very painful that the finding of one's anger in place of these emotions temporarily ameliorates such uncomfortable feelings.

The man or woman who continually rails against their partner and the world, whose capacity for contempt or for a fight is always at the ready, uses anger as a way *to break connections*. The anger may not only be a cover for other emotions, it is also a way to disavow the need for the emotional connections that the other has stirred up. That is to say, if feelings of vulnerability, disappointment or hurt are experienced as so painful that they almost can't be felt but are speedily transformed into a more manageable emotional response, then a distance has to be made from the person who has elicited those emotional responses. That distance is achieved by putting anger in between the two people. This is anger in essence as a defence, a way to say: I'm hurting, I'm bleeding, but please don't come close, don't touch me, I'm too raw, too wounded.

The problem with this kind of anger is that since it is essentially a shield against other emotions, an internal battle ensues. The person who is hurting *does* crave relating, *does* want their hurt soothed, *does* want the other to come in close, but they are scared. Worrying that more hurt will result, they daren't feel closeness and so the anger comes in its place. Moreover, this shield has to be wielded ever more frequently as the feeling it was meant to – but actually fails to – soothe threatens to break through to the surface. Here we are seeing the function of anger as a threat to connection. It disrupts the possibility of really feeling or absorbing hurt by removing one's vulnerability to another and putting in its place an automatic response of anger.

But paradoxically there is a completely opposite function to anger as well. For some people, and even for the person I've just described, at the same time as this kind of anger looks as if it separates self from other, breaks the connection and allows one to differentiate, it simultaneously provides a form of connection. What do I mean by this?

For someone who has grown up with anger as the dominant form of expression in an angry or violent household, it may have been the only medium of emotional expression which was valued or validated. If a child is often neglected and only feels related to through being told off, being shouted at on one end of the spectrum or being violated or abused at the other, the child may be confused by the meaning of relationship in the first place. Relationship has meant hurt and relationship has meant maltreatment. These are the terms in which relationship has been understood and experienced, and while another form of relationship may be longed for, it is impossible if it is unavailable.

Even when a different form of relationship is offered, it may not be possible for the person to believe in it, to trust it, to relax into a more equal, mutual relationship. It feels odd, unfamiliar as though it doesn't quite register on any known emotional scale.

The individual who is emotionally unable to assimilate mutuality, finds resonance in a relationship that mirrors familiar feeling states – states of hurt, of conflict, of isolation, of misunderstanding. There can be a kind of relief in angry or violent interchange because it enacts a form of contact that is known. It provides a crescendo or outlet – a means to intensity; a way to feel heard, or at the very least, a way to feel one is authentically expressing oneself.

But the problem with this is that intensity is misinterpreted as connection. And as this form of connection is reiterated it takes the person away from the possibility of more intimate connections. Anger stands in where a wider range of emotional states needs to be shared.

Anger Part 2

I have discussed the ways in which people can find themselves expressing anger as a response to all sorts of emotional situations that they encounter. Their anger is at the ready to defend them, to shield them from feelings they find more troublesome.

Now I want to look at the other side of the coin – not at anger as a defence, but at defences that can get in the way of the recognition and expression of legitimate anger. Many people may spend time with their families, bottling up emotions to keep the peace. Grown-up children especially can feel infantilised when they re-enter the parental environment and find themselves restricting the range of their emotional responses.

Anger is one such emotion. Anger is an emotion we can become afraid of. We think of it as a negative emotion (as though emotions can be divided up into good and bad) and we think of it as a destructive, disruptive emotion. But, we might ask, is this really so? Is anger something we need to be quite so afraid of? Where does this fear come from and is it right for us to maintain it?

Part of the fear stems from what we observe and are taught

as children. We are only comfortable with the range of emotions we are introduced to and if we are denied particular forms of emotional expression we become uneasy with identifying, recognising, accepting 'dissident' emotions. We then experience 'foreign' emotions vaguely or vicariously. A family that suppresses anger, or only allows it to come out in limited ways, conveys to its members the idea that there is something scary or wrong about feeling angry. This means that not only is there a taboo on expressing anger; there is even a taboo on recognising when one is feeling angry. Angry feelings have to be speedily converted into sets of feelings that are more tolerable.

The taboo on anger is especially – although by no means exclusively or inclusively – directed against girls. And when the directive, 'Nice girls don't get angry' is internalised, it can have damaging effects. It can act as an internal brake on a girl or woman's ability to assert herself. Wary of the consequences of feeling anger, she becomes watchful of her emotional responses in general. She restricts them to those that are acceptable; but this diminishes her capacity to be emotionally in tune with herself, to know what she feels, to feel comfortable with her emotions and to act from a knowledge of them.

For girls and women whose self-identity depends to some extent (and what woman's doesn't?) on keeping relational connections alive through their capacity to understand, to empathise and be in tune with others, indeed to focus a good deal of their attention on the emotional needs of *others*, experiencing personal needs can feel threatening. To recognise one's own needs creates a psychological separation from others. It means that our own needs do not necessarily meld with the meeting of needs in others. If one has serviced others' needs for a long time a recognition that personal needs have been ignored or trampled on – both by oneself and perhaps by others – can rouse one to anger. Recognising anger when one has been misheard, unseen, taken advantage of, is an assertion of self. This act can feel dangerous and unfamiliar.

Julia's father was given to making promises about what he

would do with her – take her to the funfair, the movies, camping – and then often letting her down. In an attempt to quell her disappointment, Mum would 'excuse' Dad and his heavy work-load or his forgetfulness. She suffered in the same way; really there was little to be done about it. Countless evenings Julia saw Mum sigh when Dad neglected to turn up. While Julia focused on poor Dad and how he was overloaded she neglected her own emotional response . . . it simply wasn't given space. When disappointed by others in her life, Julia always saw it from their point of view. She 'forgave' them, even half expecting to be let down, believing she couldn't possibly be a priority.

In therapy, it became obvious that Julia's acceptance of such disappointments, and her anticipation of the unreliability of others (especially men) rested on low self-esteem – an inability to value herself as she valued others. She didn't feel entitled to put her own responses first. To do so, to dare to feel what she was feeling rather than thinking about the other when she was let down, made her feel quite out of sorts. She felt as though she had grown too big: her feelings overwhelmed her; the anger she discovered inside herself felt like it would obliterate others; she felt she risked retaliatory rejection. Recognising her anger didn't just make her feel visible, it made her feel enormous and ungainly as though she was taking up much more space than she ought.

At the same time as she was having to cope with this enlarged picture of self, she felt that the recognition of her anger put a distance between herself and others. It was as though coming in touch with her own feelings rather than focusing on the motivations or needs of the other created a boundary between herself and the other. It was as if she was saying: I am as important as you. This act of assertion felt like a betrayal of a self-identity in which understanding of the other had been paramount. Furthermore the declaration of self implicit in the recognition of anger served to create distance and distinction. Where Julia had known herself through her capacity to identify and empathise with others, and to put their needs first, now she was confronting a self who through acceptance of the legitimacy of her own feelings was asserting difference and differentiation.

Julia was fearful that her new-found anger would find no bounds, that she would rollercoaster over others who injured or ignored her, that she would be rejected if she exposed her anger when she felt trampled on. But she found, to her surprise, that the more she allowed herself to feel angry, the more she came in touch with other powerful emotions, and her emotional range as well as the intensity of her emotions – both the pleasurable and the more painful ones – expanded. She continued to feel compassion and concern for others' points of view but she didn't privilege them above hers and she said that having access to her anger spontaneously allowed her to feel for the first time that she was living in her own life rather than adjusting to others' lives.

So paradoxically we can see that both the fear of feeling anger and the speedy arousal to anger (see 'Anger' pp. 53–56) have a common origin in our limited emotional vocabulary. When we are deprived of a full range of emotional responses we become alienated from aspects of ourselves and are forced to express ourselves through limited channels. This encourages us to feel that there is something wrong with ourselves when feelings, previously 'off limits', are stirred up. We may see anger as a defence against those feelings or we may fear anger itself as being outside our normal range. As we can risk encountering our feelings in their subtleties rather than in large brushstrokes, anger will inevitably find a role as an expressoin of neither menace nor detachment, but as an understandable response to infringement or mistreatment.

Christmas

'I'm dreading going home for Christmas. I'm 36 with my own family but my parents treat me like a child. Everyone pretends to get on but their disapproval of me and my rage at them is palpable. Help!'

Christmas in the UK now starts at the end of October. By the time Christmas Eve has arrived, many people are shopped out, partied out, carolled out and ready to escape.

For the non-religious (and even some of the religious) the festival has become more a mixture of frenzied activity, anticipation of pleasure and dread of obligation than a time of joy and reflection. The symbolic meanings of Christmas with its hopeful message of birth, renewal and salvation do entwine with the sense of community implicit in the observance of the winter solstice, but these potential pleasures are often marred by our expectations (conscious and unconscious) of Christmas and our memory of what has happened when we as families have come together to celebrate the day.

The joviality of Christmas masks many people's deep isolation and loneliness. Whether actually alone and bombarded by the synthetic merry-making emanating from every radio and TV set or feeling alone within a family or friendship network, Christmas can be particularly difficult. Referrals to psychotherapists increase at this time, the suicide rate rises, and more people arrive at hospitals as a result of drunken encounters (surely not to do with happiness).

Part of the difficulty stems from the tradition that Christmas is a family holiday. And it is the current family context that induces many people to hide what they feel to be their essential selves. If the self in the family fails to mirror the self in the world, alienation ensues. Many feel they cannot reveal the selves they now know themselves to be for fear of disapproval. And yet they wish to. They yearn to be recognised within the family, but can't imagine they will be. They long for more honesty but can't believe this is possible. Family members see one another in fixed categories, assigning apparently immutable characteristics, behaviour and attitudes to one another.

On top of this, siblings, aunts and uncles, grandparents, parents and children, who may be if not estranged then distant from one another, come together to share in a fantasy of what Christmas is. But despite the overwhelmingly homogenised public imagery detailing what constitutes The Family Christmas, we do all nevertheless retain our own personal fantasies and wishes for Christmas. We have sets of desires and hopes about what this coming together will bring.

Grown-up children wish to be seen as separate by their parents, parents wish not to be taken for granted by their children, relatives long for real engagement rather than patronising indulgence. There is nothing amiss with these wishes in themselves; the difficulty arises when we are unable to recognise them and we walk into the Family Christmas unaware of the hopes and longings we have and the potential disappointments we face.

Families who have never had a Christmas uninterrupted by rows become tense with anticipation and then find themselves almost provoking the fight to relieve this built-up tension.

Other families have a knack of forgetting about their propensity to row. When the inevitable fighting starts, instead of there being an acceptance that relating through this form of contact seems necessary, one member of the family scolds the others: 'There you go again, we can never have a peaceful time.' No one can reposition themelves: the holiday is ruined, this one has upset that one, this one has done the usual. In place of a good-humoured adaptation that recognises this family's need for a fight, there is bitterness, anger and feelings of betrayal.

At Christmas, as our reader writes, we are expected to bury the pain and get on with the jollity. But the way our expectations intersect with existing family dynamics can make for a troublesome time.

So what can we do? Trying to clear some thinking time to encounter our own expectations is probably the best preventive against disaster. If we can become aware of the images we construct, the fantasies we carry and the wishes we take with us into the family we may be able to go into Christmas feeling that we have more personal agency and are consequently less victim-ised. For some, that will mean talking with parents before the event; for others it means not screening out vital details of their current life in order to protect the other, as doing this somehow abandons the self. More self-aware, we may not necessarily get what we want but we won't let ourselves down by engaging in a charade that leaves us bereft of the desired contact from the family as well as bereft of one's self.

Promises

Three and a half weeks into January for many people means three weeks into broken resolutions. Every year on January 1st, millions of us make resolutions only to see them in tatters a few weeks later. A week of grief may follow our inability to hold to the resolutions but then we forget about them for eleven months until we gear up again in late December. What is the force of resolutions? Why are they so attractive to us? What are they about, and why are we so often destined to break them and remake them anew each year? What is the inner psychological struggle that can occur when a resolution is made?

Resolutions are as often as not resolutions to stop a particular behaviour – to give up smoking; not to eat sweets; to stop biting one's nails; to cease running up credit card debts; not to let work pile up; to listen more and shout less. They are an attempt to change behaviour that we find disagreeable yet which cannot be given up without considerable effort. The making of a resolution marks the significance of the attempt: it marks the act out as special, as requiring a particular effort.

In this sense we could say that resolutions serve a positive function. They consciously imply a commitment to transformation. They take problem x as serious enough to need attention and they give the individual the space to think about a habitual type of behaviour so that they can make a conscious choice about engaging in it rather than pursuing it thoughtlessly. But the very reason why x behaviour has become entrenched is the very reason why simply removing it is almost destined to fail.

Behaviour we find uncomfortable or disagreeable, acts on our part that embarrass or displease us, that feel out of our control, unpredictable or just plain uncomfortable, exist for a reason. They don't just occur serendipitously. We smoke or bite our nails or are cruel for complex reasons, and removing offending behaviour like a surgeon excising a tumour doesn't work.

When we decide to remove or banish a behaviour we are saying, in effect, 'This aspect of me is bad; I must rid myself of it.' This relation to self and this concept about good and bad bits of self reflect a generally held cultural idea of the human being as divided between good and evil. It is an outgrowth of certain Judaeo-Christian teachings that have found their way into philosophy, pop psychology and of course self-experience. It poses an inevitable struggle between these two aspects of self where the observing self needs to maintain a vigilance so that the bad bits don't overwhelm us.

But how useful is this as a concept? Of course it is possible to produce behavioural change in the short term but if we are looking for longer-lasting change, and change that won't induce another type of behaviour which is equally distressing, then it is pretty useless. For having designated a part of self as bad, several things occur which bypass an understanding of its possible functions.

Most importantly, in characterising x behaviour as bad we are attempting to stifle it. When behaviours, activities and desires are banished, we all know well how extra attractive and compelling they can become. It is similar with emotions. When we are discouraged from expressing a feeling, when we encounter someone who has decided that he or she mustn't show sadness, we are struck by the falsity of their good humour; it just doesn't ring true. The very mechanism of deprivation eventually sets up its counterpoint. In the short term, of course, banishing chocolates or whatever gives one a feeling of strength. One has withstood temptation, put oneself firmly on the side of good and affirmed a commitment to the 'good' self, to not needing x. When the desire for chocolates asserts itself, one redoubles one's efforts and gets a quick high from being able to refuse, to be able to see oneself as capable of self-denial. This ability to deny becomes the substitute pleasure. We feel good *because* of our capacity to override our desire, to stare it in the face and do battle with it.

This temporary high is at the cost of dividing oneself into bits; of treating aspects of self as an enemy to be tamed. More significantly, however, it prevents us from discovering what on earth the apparently offending behaviour is about. Why is it there, what is it doing for us? Is it an aberration or does it contain some symbolic meaning?

What is needed to hold the resolution in place is not simply disengagement from the behaviour but a simultaneous active engagement with its meaning. We need to explore what it represents; what it tells us about ourselves; what it encapsulates. Types of behaviour – agreeable or disagreeable – exist for reasons which if decoded can provide the basis for more long-lasting change.

Brian decided to stop smoking for the New Year. He had done this several times before but three months on he'd find himself smoking again. He returned to the familiar habit when a crisis hit: the last one had been when his girlfriend had had a miscarriage. He said cigarettes seemed to give him something certain in a time of confusion and uncertainty. But is that really what is going on? How do cigarettes soothe Brian's sad, scary feelings following his girlfriend's miscarriage?

The cigarettes served the function not of soothing the feelings, but of legitimising Brian's right to be upset. The cigarettes symbolised the upset. Without them as a vehicle he felt uneasy about expressing or exposing his upset to his girlfriend, his friends or himself. He felt he shouldn't really be that upset. It was useless. He was in conflict about the rightness of his feelings and smoking shifted that problem to one of feeling sorry for himself for engaging in what he considered a self-destructive behaviour – smoking.

Once he had engaged with the purpose of the smoking, Brian had more understanding of what it did for him. It had become a circuitous route for emotional expression of feelings of sadness and powerlessness; feelings he was uneasy with in the normal course of events; feelings he berated himself for in general because they were unproductive.

Feelings, of course, are not good, bad, productive or unproductive. They simply are. Why we feel a particular way given a particular set of circumstances is of course analysable. Often we discover that our initial feeling hides other feelings that are felt for one reason or another to be unmanageable. When we can accept and understand a feeling, we can sense some power in relation to that feeling, but as long as we feel embarrassed about it, guilty for having it or overwhelmed by it we will do all we can to get rid of it.

Resolutions to do away with behaviour, which could more accurately be read as injunctions not to feel, will almost inevitably fail. What is needed in place of resolution is the recognition of the need that we feel must be squashed. If that need can be brought to light it stands a chance of being psychologically accommodated, even if it can't easily be met. When Brian could allow himself to mourn the lost baby, to stop feeling it was his fault (it wasn't) and to find a part of himself that could be compassionate rather than stoical, he could desist from smoking. He could digest his feelings rather than ceaselessly having to puff them away.

Envy

We routinely experience feelings without understanding what is included in them. Jealousy, I suggest in another article, is a mechanism that plays into already existing feelings of insecurity which make it hard to believe that one is loved and cared for. Male violence towards women often conceals great feelings of vulnerability, feelings that cause such discomfort that they get transposed into fury, not dissimilar to the ways in which complex emotional hungers of all kinds become translated into food and body image obsessions.

I want to consider the emotion of envy. Frequently aroused but often hard to accept, it can feel degrading and impoverishing. We live in a society in which great disparities between people exist and have always existed. Our socialisation, until very recently, taught us to accept our place, not to want what was above our station, to accept the rightness of a society divided by class, gender and race.

Envy in these circumstances is seen as an unfortunate blot on the character. It is felt that one should be able to tolerate difference without feeling hard done by, otherwise one is exposing personal meanness and small-mindedness.

But envy (and indeed anger) is a predictable outcome of a situation in which structural arrangements create great gaps between what people have. And this envy – whether of an individual, a group, a gender, a race or a class, and what they have in terms of social privilege, wealth, access and so on – hurts on several levels simultaneously.

First, one comes into touch with one's feelings of deprivation. We become aware of the feelings aroused by the emotional, material or physical lacks that are so unjust. Then one can feel diminished and shameful. Feelings of envy create a pinched, ungenerous sense of self. The distaste this kind of feeling arouses can be extremely difficult, especially if one feels envy towards a friend. These feelings can threaten or poison a friendship, so that on top of the envy there is loss.

Lastly – and perhaps this is the bit that causes so much difficulty – the feelings called forth about that envied other are often extremely mean, destructive and hateful. We may find ourselves wishing the other misfortune. Or, if they appear to have something that we judge is not rightly theirs, there may be a secret wish that they will fall on their face and get their comeuppance.

This latter set of feelings – the harmful wishes towards another – is what stands in the way, for many, of exploring our envy. We may berate ourselves for feeling so ungiving and spiteful. And we may do our damnedest to get rid of the feelings, to push them aside, to forget them or somehow rid ourselves of them.

But what really is going on when we feel envy? Is there another way to understand the enormous discomfort it causes?

Jenny and Marie are senior social workers. Both feel stuck in their jobs, burdened by managerial responsibilities, misunderstood by the public and undersupported by the teams they lead. They commiserate and fantasise together. One evening, over supper, Marie tells Jenny of her plans to set up a consultancy service in her speciality: childhood sexual abuse. She talks excitedly and quite concretely. Jenny can see that Marie has thought all this out rather well, but at the same time as she feels impressed with Marie's plans and pleased for her she notices a *frisson* of envy erupting inside her. By the end of the meal, Jenny can hardly eat. She feels positively uncomfortable, contaminated by feelings of envy she doesn't know how to handle or think about.

Jenny feels guilty for being so stingy and self-involved. In an attempt to divert herself from those feelings she keeps up a cheery exterior, asking Marie lots of questions about the proposed consultancy. She goes home feeling awful: why didn't she think of that? Why does Marie have all the good ideas? Why do things come so easily to her? If ony she were more like Marie. As she berates herself, she feels a great gulf opening between her and Marie.

But what is going on here? Why such overwhelming feelings of envy? What is their function, and what do they tell us about Jenny and Marie?

Let's recall the situation. Neither Marie nor Jenny was happy in her job. They commiserated and felt a kind of bonding, even an enmeshment, that reinforced both of them and assuaged the dreaded gloomy feelings that often came over them. They understood one another, were in a similar situation and could moan together about their predicament. Marie's plan to start a consultancy suddenly threw this pattern of relating into question. Jenny felt abandoned, alone with her own difficulties. The envy she was experiencing was in some sense about loss – an anticipated loss of understanding, a distance she saw opening up between her and Marie. But beyond this, Jenny found Marie's capacity to think herself into and create a new situation intimidating. She despaired about ever being able to find such a solution for herself.

For Jenny, the envy concealed deep feelings of wanting to express her own needs and desires that were entangled with equally strong feelings of prohibition. Her desires were so often foiled almost before they could be experienced. A profound sense of unentitlement thwarted her capacity to find out about her own needs. What she envied in Marie was not Marie's plans *per se*, but the fact that, as Jenny saw it, Marie managed to know and then act on her desires. In other words the envy was not about the actuality of Marie's situation. It was a signal of Jenny's own distress about the difficulty she experienced with desire.

What Jenny needed to do was to use the signal of envy to try and explore her own conflict about desire; to hold on to and struggle with her fears, her tentativeness, her anxieties about her entitlement to want. When she could do that, when she could pull her feelings back into herself rather than projecting them on to her friend, she was able to engage with her fears and begin the process of daring to feel and actualise her own wants.

Meanwhile Marie was not untouched by Jenny's emotional reaction. Although it was unspoken she registered it, and it caused her to feel shaky. She too experienced discomfort pursuing her desires. As she focused on Jenny's reaction the discomfort shifted from her psychological difficulties with allowing herself to follow through with her plan to feeling guilty that she was abandoning Jenny, to feeling angry that in some subtle way Jenny was trying to hold her back. In this way she undermined herself until she could pull back and refocus on her own desires and the problems she had sticking with them.

But, perhaps you may be asking, this begs the question of why Jenny and Marie both felt so shaky about their sense of entitlement. Briefly, it stemmed from similar experiences in which both felt that their wants consistently went unrecognised. This lack of acceptance had come to make them feel – in differing degrees – that there was something wrong with them for wanting.

This pattern was more intense in Jenny's case. She both disavowed knowing her needs and repressed the pain of having been unrecognised. She could then feel her need to want only in relation to *another's desire*. She could not easily feel it for herself.

With this understanding, envy, rather than creating an indigestible ambience, could become a sign to Jenny (and to a lesser extent to Marie) that conflict about desire needs to be engaged with. Envy instead of being a dreaded emotion could be rehabilitated. Jenny could see it as an opportunity to appreciate that her desires were still very much alive and that she needed to find a way to express them.

Jealousy

Jealousy is one of the most unpleasant feelings in the world. One feels suspicious, distrustful and mean. One feels threatened. Desperately insecure. Guilty at one's possessiveness. Alternately angry and clingy. We feel so powerless, so overcome that the only soothing that seems possible is to want the person who has provoked the feeling to renounce all interest in the outside world and to focus on us.

Feelings of jealousy can occur in a variety of circumstances. What distinguishes jealousy from its cousin envy is that whereas envy is often about a two-person situation – 'I envy her job; his lifestyle; his house; her beauty' – jealousy is engendered in threes. We feel jealous of a partner's friendships and activities outside the relationship; jealous of one's child's affection for its step-parent; jealous of the attention a sibling receives from the parent.

There is, in jealousy, a perceived loss of affection. We feel that the attention our friend, colleague or partner is giving a third party or activity – going down the pub, rock climbing, going off to professional conferences, talking to someone attractive at a party – is attention that is being withheld from us. It is as though what one requires and what is one's due is being stolen by the third party. Without that third party or activity we feel we would be free of the debilitating feelings of insecurity that jealousy engenders.

Jealousy first becomes part of our emotional vocabulary when we are young and we sense a situation in which we fear or experience loss. The arrival of a sibling is usually accompanied by much hoo-ha and pleasure in the wider community. All attention is focused on the baby, and the first-born is greeted with an onslaught of statements from the surrounding adults that mischaracterise her or his experience. 'Aren't you happy to have a sister to play with?', 'Isn't he sweet.' 'Help Mummy now; don't be difficult.'

But such unthinking comments desperately miss the experience of first-born children. For, from their perspective, this good event has only brought problems and confusion. Everything has changed. He or she is shunted to one side. An incredible period of adjustment is in process. There is much grief and loss and anger about the baby intruder. There are wishes that the baby be taken away, that the equilibrium be restored, that he or she could once again be the baby in the family.

Such jealousy is an expected developmental step. If we can keep in mind that the older child feels loss, and feels resentment at having to adjust to the new expanded family, if we can allow children to articulate their jealousy, then other feelings, positive feelings about being a sibling have a chance to grow rather than being gnarled up by the need to deny jealousy. If jealous feelings can be handled in this way they shouldn't give us many problems in later life. Although we will be vulnerable to jealous feelings when we perceive a potential loss, they will pass as we accustom ourselves to new and changed circumstances.

But if such losses are consistently unacknowledged, if we can't bear to see the child's pain, to accept its fears and allow its direct articulations of the loss but instead criticise the child for showing its feelings and entreat it to deny these feelings, then a much more troublesome scenario is in store. Then the feelings of insecurity caused by the loss and feelings of jealousy will combine to be rekindled at other times of loss and change. Such a person develops little sense that loss is part of life. They only see that loss is disastrous. Jealous reactions become an attempt to obliterate that truth. To deny the pain of the loss, to turn back the clock, to undo what has been done.

The question the jealous child and the jealous adult seek to have answered is: 'Do you still love me?' And if that question can't be addressed, our insecurity increases. Acute jealous reactions can occur, which in turn lead one to interpret all sorts of situations as foretelling betrayal and loss. Jealousy becomes an *externalisation* of internally felt insecurity. As we focus on the *other* we place the solution outside ourselves. We hope that the object of our jealousy can be removed and with it the feeling of insecurity.

A woman finds herself extremely jealous of her husband's activities in a local choir. The choir meets every Wednesday evening and more frequently when they are rehearsing for a performance. Every Wednesday evening either before or after choir there is considerable tension between the two of them. The wife feels menaced. Rationally she tells herself there is nothing to worry about. It's not even that she feels lonely on those evenings for she has plenty of independent activities of her own. But emotionally she is in agony. She is worried about the other women, their interest in her husband, his interest in them. She finds it hard to believe and trust his commitment to her and she imagines infidelity and treachery.

For his part the husband is irritated. He feels impinged upon but at the same time culpable as though there is indeed something wrong in his wanting to do something apart from his work outside the marriage. Instead of acknowledging the importance of the choir and his need to have separate activities while reassuring his wife of his continuing need of her and connection to her, he acts like a guilty man slinking off to a mistress. And he provokes her further by failing to tell her in advance of additional choir practice and musical weekends.

Both people in this couple are (in their encounter with one another) dealing with historically established feelings of insecurity. Her insecurity about his love of her which would have surfaced at some point in the relationship now has a third party – jealousy – as an avenue for expression. She seeks reassurance but instead her insecurity is fuelled by her partner's inability to acknowledge the Wednesday evening/performance/weekend/ separations. The man is like the parent who pretends that the new baby is of no consequence; instead of offering reassurance he backs away, thus unwittingly stoking up her insecurity and her jealousy. Or is it so unwitting? For her insecurity, her jealousy – inconvenient and annoying though it is – allows him to feel wanted and secure. He is not required to admit to himself his need or his vulnerability. As long as *she* expresses the distress, as long as *she* is the one who wants him to relinquish his other activities, then he is able to negate his own feelings of insecurity and avoid the struggle with how he manages closeness and separateness within the relationship.

What the woman really needs to be investigating for herself is why the loss of her husband on these occasions *feels* like abandonment. She needs to be able to show him her vulnerability directly, to have their differing needs acknowledged and to receive from him a sense that his activity is not a sneaky thing but an important part of his life that is not in conflict with his love of her. And the man needs to investigate for himself why he feels the need to sneak off to choir practice and why he finds it difficult to reassure his partner.

The vulnerabilities we feel when we are close are sometimes hard to contain. We seek all sorts of defensive ruses to conceal the depth of our attachments, from a feigned lack of interest, to attack on and contempt for the other's activities, to the taking up of falsely independent behaviour. But jealousy is another mechanism that feeds the fear of intimacy. In many painful ways we believe ourselves to be unlovable and when and if we find love we often can't believe it. We test it, treat it with scorn, refuse or do not know how to enjoy it. Jealousy in this context becomes a defensive manoeuvre – a focus on an external threat when what is required is engagement with the internal difficulty of trusting.

Stress

Stress is something we are all familiar with. Some of us thrive on it, some of us abhor it, while some of us are able to accept that it is just part of life. In stressful periods our adrenalin seems to pump through us at great speed. After the stress-inducing factors have receded we may feel exhausted, in need of rest and recuperation, or just grateful that we are back in step with ourselves again. But what of those of us who seem continually in a state, who seem to need to be wound up, to encounter life as a series of dramas? What is the internal experience, and what is the psychological function of living in a whirlwind of crisis?

John, a successful architect in his early forties, was continually swamped by the details of running a practice. Correspondence with clients and contractors, cash-flow problems, finishing dates and a schedule which involved deft juggling meant he was in a morass of overwork and chaos. Although the stress this created in him was wearing, at the same time part of him recognised that he seemed to need the intensity that living from crisis to crisis created. He felt alive in it. The demands upon him were heightened and his ability to respond made him feel powerful.

It was as though without this level of stress his life felt empty. He felt he wasn't quite real.

So what was going on here? John was successful at his job, he loved designing, he was well thought of and got lots of commissions. Yet he seemed to be harassed by people requiring responses from him which he delayed fulfilling. At one level John was quite capable of dealing with his correspondence, drawings, specs and billings. But his inability to keep on top of these essential aspects of his work served a function; gave him something. If he could discover what that was he might be able to change the level of stress he lived with.

John felt uneasy producing drawings or specifications unless he was under pressure. In order to produce he required a mental state akin to combat. Creating within a relatively calm space failed to motivate him. So hyping up the demands on himself, and structuring a situation in which he was swamped and somewhat overwhelmed, gave him the conditions he felt he needed in order to work. But paradoxically, his inability to deal with the details of his work took up so much time and produced so much worry that it impinged on his ability to do the work he actually liked. He felt trapped.

In exploring this conflict John discovered that by creating this chaos and tension he was responding to a negative view of himself. Since his schooldays the idea that he wasn't really that good or original and wouldn't amount to much had lodged inside him, almost goading him. At the same time there was an aspect of himself which rejected that view and which provided the fuel to mobilise his creativity. But it was as though he could only create out of the embattled emotional state. If people were always ringing him because they needed something or he had failed to do something they required, he had a frequent reminder that he was valued, that he was needed, that he was wanted. He could then mobilise that part of himself for himself. The external validation was like a salve to the inner experience of low self-worth.

On a deeper level, this kind of stress, which serves the function of making one feel alive, needed and purposeful, frequently masks more difficult feelings. In many cases the absence of stress can expose feelings of emptiness, of a deep internal void, of feeling that one is nothing. Such feelings are extremely difficult. By surrounding oneself with constant frenetic activity the affected person can keep such potentially paralysing, incapacitating feelings from coming into consciousness.

But in the long term the effects of stress are debilitating. Keeping up an optimum tension is not feasible. Too much stress is finally engulfing and destroys the ability to be creative. As long as such a person believes that their creativity comes out of doing battle with a negative self-image, they will be trapped. If they can recognise that their creativity is an aspect of self – albeit one originally developed to defeat low self-esteem – then they can begin to rely on it being there for them under ordinary conditions. Once they build up confidence that this is so it becomes possible to restructure stressful work practices, because they are no longer needed.

Such a process of discovery requires not so much a historical investigation into how the person has come to feel this way – although that can be important and useful – but the recognition that the person is trying to manage an internal conflict, the stress serving to mask and solve it at the same time. When we see someone apparently wedded to stress the question to ask is: could the stress be an attempt to hide and solve an unrecognised conflict?

John wondered whether he could exist without the internal battle. Could he create, could he feel valued if he was fighting a part of himself? Once he realised how caught up he was in this internal battle, he found 'creating' really quite effortless and enjoyable. It wasn't at all the tortured activity that he had fictionalised it to be. It was having to set up the tension that was creating the torture, not the work itself. But that realisation in turn alarmed him, for if being creative turned out to be easy for him, then it reinforced the idea that he wasn't of much value. He didn't really have to work at it and that made him feel somewhat fraudulent. He'd seen the pain his father, a poet, lived with; he knew how tortured were the real artists and creators. If it came so easy to him he must be a fake, or his work must be of insignificant value.

When John could face the fact that he enjoyed the creative aspects of his work and that he liked the technical problems they posed, he could see that his negative, embattled self-definition could be questioned. He needed to move from proving his competence and worth to accepting that he was able. If he could accept this then he had less need to rely on setting up an embattled situation in order to assert his ability, neither did he need to seek continual approval from others in the form of their need of him. He also needed to jettison an image in which creativity was elevated to a special and necessarily tortured activity. He needed to accept that for him it was just a capacity, and not one that needed to be enshrined with torment. Accepting the capacity would, in turn, reduce his reliance on intensity as a means of self-connection for he would be able to express himself through his work directly.

John's engagement with these ideas changed his stress level. He was no longer dependent on duress to provide the conditions for his work or his self-worth. Where we often think of stress as an external pressure – which it often is – it is worth looking at the internal pressures that propel us to seek it and to see whether we might not be covering up some conflict, which if uncovered could reduce its intensity.

Holidays

Holidays have an emotional kinship to Christmas. For many
many people both are anticipated for a long time, thought
about, talked about, planned for, worried over or excitedly
awaited, then finally enjoyed or endured. Romance, change,
family fun, getting away, 'indulging', rest and relaxation all
rank high as priorities sought in holidays. But often these
planned-for desires come unstuck in ways that leave us eager to
return home to 'normal' life.

Holidays are above all a break from routine. They provide a
time for relaxed reflection and review, often marking the end of
one phase of the yearly cycle and the beginning of another. As a
transition point the holiday reinvigorates our spirits and bodies.
But that is the ideal. For many, holidays can disappoint and
create tension. To have a good time one needs to be able to give
up control, examining and adjusting expectations as one goes
along.

Let's look at three common scenarios – the family holiday;
the lovers' holiday; the friends' holiday – in which control issues
of one kind or another can interfere with the requirements of a
holiday frame of mind.

The family holiday contains many different germs of potential disappointment. Structurally, the family is a unit and together in a new environment. This dreamed of, but *uncommon*, state of affairs requires readjustment on the part of everyone. First of all the grown-ups are spending much more time together than usual and there is often an assumption of togetherness which includes the blurring of everyday roles and responsibilities. But this assumption can clash with a delicately balanced routine that works at home, and even if there is disgruntlement with the home routine, adherence to it provides a certain safety in which all parties coexist.

For example, Neil is a conventional working father who is often at his office desk before the children have left for school. By the time he returns home from work his wife, Diana, has supervised the children's homework, dealt with their problems, fed them, sorted out their transportation needs for the next day and prepared an evening meal for Neil and herself. She is resentful about the little time he spends in the domestic sphere but begrudgingly accepts the constraints of his job and the needs of the family. Her greatest wish on holiday is to have his participation in the family, to give up some of the responsibility for continual decision-making and to abandon cooking and other domestic chores.

But Diana finds the transition to togetherness difficult. She longs to unburden herself of responsibility, and to some extent she can, but she veers between abdicating it all and feeling furious that Neil isn't looking after the children properly, making sure they have their sunscreen on or aren't eating too many ice-creams. She finds it hard to give up her resentment and her control and to participate with Neil in jointly steering the holiday. This is compounded by Neil's fantasy of what being with the family entails and his tendency to impose his agenda on the holiday as though he were still a manager in the office. He is unused to the rhythm of family life and feels excluded from the ambience his wife and children have created together. He responds by initiating numerous activities until eventually his children rebel. They don't want to drive in the hot car to see x and y monument and museum; eat quietly and show exemplary manners in this mustn't-miss restaurant; climb higher and higher peaks. Holidays for the children aren't so much about achievements and ticking activities off as about hanging out with parents around. Lacking control, they respond by forming a little protest movement, rendering the whole proposition unworkable.

Lovers who don't live together and who have never spent continuous time together can encounter another kind of difficulty on holiday. Fantasies of seamless romantic time bump into an unacknowledged reality. Part of the ease of being with each other has been the conjunction of two different phenomena: their togetherness is predicated on the possibility (and actuality) of retreat to personal space, and at the same time their own personal space provides each partner with the security and safety to be generous with the other in sharing their home and making the other welcome. This is very different from being on new territory, neither guest not host but confronted with finding hotels and restaurants in a foreign country where every decision is a potential negotiation. Where each one was accustomed to relaxing in the feeling of being looked after by the other on their home ground, they are now together, and decisions about the time and the ways to enjoy it become a different proposition. The excitement of a joint venture or the struggle for control can then ensue.

An example where neither of the couple knows quite what control to exert is that of two families holidaying together in a house rented in the Dordogne. The holiday – conceived of with pleasure and as a way for children and parents who enjoyed each other greatly as friends to spend extended time together – was dogged by control issues several times a day. While both families were excellent hosts in their own households, each of the grown-ups was extremely strong-willed and had definite ideas about how to shop, what to cook, and what to do each day. And even if they didn't have strong ideas they tended to act reactively to the suggestion of the other so that disagreements and polarisations appeared regularly. Because they were good friends they could laugh at the absurdity of it all, but when they were all in thrall to the impetus to control, their communications systems became entirely unworkable and caused tremendous distress to all the adults. One minute one couple was rowing, another moment the women were in cahoots against the men, on other occasions one couple bonded together against the other couple. Several months later when the couples had recovered their equilibrium, they came to the view that holidaying together in this way posed all the problems and transitions that couples becoming a unit go through without any of the accompanying social ritual, sanction or indeed commitment to iron out or accommodate differences that emerge on such a short-term basis. While each family, like the lovers, felt welcomed in each other's home, creating a holiday space together was awkward; and that unfamiliar awkwardness with each other instead of being recognised and dealt with became transformed into a struggle for control.

The awkwardness of changed circumstances is often disregarded in the excitement of planning a holiday, but our responses to it can be a significant cause of distress. If we can see that the awkwardness is a version of shyness, and if we can be charmed rather than appalled by it, if we can use the opportunity to see that the awkwardness tells us that we have a chance to discover ourselves in a different light – which is after all one of the most refreshing aspects of a holiday – then it can bring a sweet touch to new encounters. But if we so fear that awkwardness that we subsume it under the attempt to control, we lose not just the chance to enjoy ourselves but the chance to change and experience ourselves, our relationships and our environment anew. Control may be what we resort to when we feel fearful, nervous or shy. We need to know the areas we feel we absolutely must have control over so that we can give it up in other areas.

Rest and regeneration happen when we can resist the need to

control and let ourselves feel unfamiliar feelings. On holiday our changed circumstances give us the chance to respond with wonder at our ability to experience things differently. If we remember that one important reason for going on holiday is to relinquish the control that may be necessary during the year we may be able to relax and regenerate emotionally as well as physically and have the chance to enjoy dealing with the unfamiliar events that holidays are meant to provide.

Repetition

'My mother married an American and moved away from Scotland and her family. When I was 5 and my brother 3, my father died. I was brought up in the States and moved here to marry my husband, who has just left me. My daughter is just 5 and my son 8. My husband's father deserted his family when he was 8. The synchronicity of this makes me wonder if this could possibly all be chance?'

It is often the case that we find ourselves repeating or reproducing aspects of our own family history even when we have vowed to do everything possible to avoid walking in our parents' footsteps.

Because of her experience of abandonment, Clare, the writer of the above letter, felt a strong need for a partner who was stable. When she became involved with Jim, they made a powerful alliance based partly on their shared experiences of being fatherless. When Jim left Clare when her daughter was 5, at exactly the same age as Clare had lost her father, she was very shaken. While trying to come to terms with the break-up of her marriage, she became terribly aware of the fact that she was most concerned about her daughter Kate. She agonised about the effect it was having on her, berated herself for not having known how to keep the marriage together for Kate's sake, and felt she knew what Kate was going through.

Clare felt the loss as though she were the 5-year-old. Her own experience of being a grown woman losing her marriage was overshadowed by her identification with her daughter. And although at first glance this might seem rather odd – a displacement of her own pain – in fact more complex processes were at work.

When she had been a girl herself, Clare's experience had been eclipsed by that of her mother. She had been acutely aware of her mother's misery and fragility and felt she had to hold her up, keep her going and look after her. This childhood perception meant that Clare's own distress at losing both the mother she knew before her father died, and her father, were subsumed under Clare's notion that she needed to be strong. She experienced the change in her mother but never grieved for her father (and her family life) directly.

Her identification with Kate made her aware of her need to be mindful of the children's experience of the loss of their father. But it also gave her an opportunity to find some of the feelings she had been unable to experience for herself when her own father had died.

Now as she understood the basis of her identification with Kate she could give herself the emotional space to reconnect with her own early loss and her present confusions, as well as make the space for her children to have their own experience of their father's departure. They didn't have to be strong for her and she could separate her experience from theirs, thus allowing them age-appropriate emotional responses.

Her ties with her mother had been so intense that Clare had, quite unwittingly, retraced the outlines of her life. She now began to think about how it was that she too had moved countries to marry and how she didn't seem to be able to be in a marriage that continued, albeit for very different reasons.

She realised that her early experience was like a template of what was possible for her; but it was also a way to somehow legitimise her mother's life. In reproducing certain aspects of it, Clare found a sort of reassurance. She was finding security in something she had an emotional knowledge of. She had lived her life with the overwhelming presence of her mother's pain but in connecting with that pain and with her mother's life she felt a place and a sense of self. To have had more might have been strangely disconcerting. She needed to become conscious, aware of the template before she could allow herself to have more than her mother.

Her husband's inability to stay in the family also embodied points of identification with his own early history. Although he left the marriage he was determined to have an active relationship with his children – he didn't want them to be cut off from their father the way he was. However, he felt impelled to leave the marriage partly because he carried no internal picture of the possibility of a harmonious family with two parents. But he was also identifying with the imagined father who had left him so inexplicably and so painfully. In leaving the family he was somehow linking with his own father, trying to make connections with him, trying to fill in the void and in a complex way feel himself into his father's shoes and discover the allure of leaving. He had no awareness of a positive image of his father, but knew that in leaving his wife and children he was on a search to find a part of himself that had died when his father had left.

Instances of repeating familial experiences are common, not just in personal life but in work life too. Jake, the son of an outwardly successful and charismatic musician who in later life was disgraced when it was revealed that he was having sexual relations with young boys, built a career for himself in the law. Since turning 40 he'd found himself drinking worryingly. He'd always disdained his father's weakness and was sure that he would be able to be more in control of his impulses.

Since he'd become a QC Jake would find himself subject to

sudden and incomprehensible panics. Something was wrong but he couldn't name it or understand it. His life was going well and his work was going well but for the panic attacks. His turn to drinking could be understood as a fear of competing with his father. But this explanation, while comfortably fulfilling the expectation of the Oedipal drama, missed the more potent issue: Jake's difficulty in imagining for himself what he had not experienced – success without disaster.

It wasn't that he couldn't surpass his father that caused the problems; it was the shame he internalised about his father's difficulty. Jake came to know about his father's problems with the rest of the world when they became public. But long before the public humiliation, Jake had sponged up the emotional ambience in the family. He had sensed some dis-ease that was never spoken about, some distress associated with his father, and so he had grown up with a sense that success and creativity at work were bundled together with distress in a messy burden. His own success then invoked an unknown dis-ease, which until he could face it found expression in panic attacks and drinking.

Our drive to repeat difficult aspects of our parents' lives stems, then, not so much from the events themselves – death, loss, public humiliation – but from a felt (unconscious) obligation to carry aspects of our parents' experience that had become unmanageable to them. Clare's and Jake's parents' feelings of shame and loss crowded the emotional space without being digested in such a way that Clare and Jake could find their own emotional responses. They were placed in the position of holding their mother's or their father's feelings and then, in an attempt to integrate with their own experience, recreating similar circumstances in order to reconnect with their personal feelings.

When parents find it hard to acknowledge their feelings and take responsibility for them, children have a hard time feeling their own. The drive to repeat becomes a way to make that space, to catch up with parts that became split off when not understood earlier in life.

Denial

There has been a fairly wide-ranging attack on both the efficacy of psychotherapy and on therapists who are said to have misled their patients into falsely believing that they have been sexually abused in childhood.

An organisation defending the rights of those who believe that they have been falsely accused of sexual abuse has been formed. It claims that a new syndrome, False Memory Syndrome (FMS), is in place. In this argument it is said that naive patients are encouraged by psychotherapists to believe that the distress and anger they feel are consistent with childhood sexual abuse. The therapist is charged with reconstructing the patient's memory in such a way that the individual believes that they were abused when this was not the case.

Undoubtedly there are therapists who, recognising the catalogue of distress symptoms that coalesce around a person who has been abused, suggest the possibility of childhood sexual abuse to their clients or patients. Indeed a therapist who is not prepared to consider this possibility is doing their patients or clients a great disservice. Childhood sexual abuse exists in great numbers of people so can be expected to appear in a proportion of those who are in therapy. But, of course, there may be therapists who through a variety of means misconstrue a situation and, instead of helping their clients to find a way of understanding their distress, have drawn up a programme of confrontation or suggested that actual physical abuse occurred when instead there was an emotional ambience of abuse. This practice is irresponsible and must be addressed.

However, the passion aroused by FMS leads me to take up three points. I want to discuss the process of therapy and the problems of repression. Secondly, I want to address how psychotherapy has been seen as simultaneously whitewashing sexual abuse and yet exaggerating its occurrence. Thirdly I want to talk about the attack on feminism and on the veracity of widespread sexual abuse.

As a therapist who has practised from the time in which sexual abuse in childhood was first denied (or seen as very, very exceptional) to a time when its widespread appearance made it imperative that clinicians review their cases to make sure they weren't missing a history of abuse, the intriguing aspect to me is the suggestion that one can easily convince someone in therapy that events have occurred that haven't.

Therapy is not about convincing or arguing a point. Certainly the therapist, in order to be of use to an individual, has to have a point of view. The therapist listens, observes and offers to the client a tentative understanding of the meaning of the client's actions, thoughts and feelings. The client then corrects, concurs, modifies and puts into her or his own words what seems accurate. Together the therapist and client hone ways of understanding which develop and change in the course of the therapy.

One of the enormous difficulties one bears witness to as a psychotherapist is the struggle of a client to avoid encountering aspects of their experience that are unwanted. Repression of painful experience is a mighty force. It can't simply be lifted off to reveal a truth. Even when events can be considered crystal clear and it seems there is no room for misinterpretation, the individual can render the situation in a variety of different ways.

We all have the ability to split off and keep from ourselves aspects of unwanted experience. This phenomenon is actively explored in therapy. But it doesn't mean that because there is the space to investigate split-off experience, an individual embraces the opportunity. The ability to split off, disassociate from and repress experience is related to the damaging aspects of that experience. If past experiences are benign they are held in an accessible form; if they are consistently cruel they may not be remembered or they may exist behind a screen that serves to hide the more problematic memories. If cruelty has been observed and acknowledged by another then the individual tends to have more access to it. But it is when the cruelty is hidden or denied, when the abuse or torture occurs behind closed doors and outside the knowledge of others, that it tends to be split off most severely.

In my experience and the experience of many of my colleagues, clients with a history of sexual abuse or sexual torture, clients with considerable hidden violence in their background, are very, very frightened to acknowledge it. When it feels almost obvious to the therapist, the client may not be able to see it. This is similar to mechanisms that come into play when someone in a repetitively bad relationship fails to recognise the invented world she or he lives in to protect themself from its reality.

Repeated abuse produces a range of responses that enable the person to continue to live within the situation they find themselves in. These include the capacity to repress and deny to oneself the reality of the abuse. They also include great feelings of shame, great rage, low self-worth and a sense of having been the perpetrator oneself. These responses make it hard for people to take on the idea that they have been abused. They are often deeply appalled by the notion and resist it on both a rational and a psychological level. To claim that such people are highly suggestible is inconsistent with and opposes responsible clinical experience.

If people are fabricating sexual abuse then one wonders what kind of psychological difficulty they are in for them to require this particular legitimation of their pain. If they are misnaming the source of their distress we need to provide them with help that more accurately reflects the cause of their pain.

The second point arising out of the attack on therapy is rather ironic. The Freudian heritage has whitewashed cases of sexual abuse, substituting not a denial of the abuse itself but a denial of its significance and the privileging instead of unconscious fantasy and desire. The conflation of two very different ideas – childhood sexual fantasy and sexual abuse as fantasy – has always been problematic in psychoanalysis. Sexual abuse is about a coercive relationship in which power, cruelty and sadism are at work. Sexual fantasy, on the other hand, is about the longings a child has to reposition itself *vis-à-vis* the Oedipal constellation and to disrupt the power relations in the family in which children can feel excluded from the parental couple. There is a world of difference between the two which cannot be mistaken in the clinical situation.

My third point relates to the current attack on feminism. Many accounts have asserted that those in the grip of FMS are feminists. The use of this kind of political baiting to cast doubt on survivors' memories is surely no coincidence. Feminism was the political movement that highlighted the importance of the personal, the subjective experience in everyday life. Feminism made it possible for women to speak of their experiences of the gender divide and in doing so forced us all to confront deeply troubling aspects of our cultural and psychic life. Feminism insisted that we listen and that we talk, and in that talking widespread sexual abuse was uncovered. As women claimed the right to be subjects, they claimed those same rights for children.

Is the call to support FMS now to be part of the backlash against feminism? Is FMS a new stick to beat feminism with as well as a device to aid the endemic denial of sexual abuse in our society?

Betrayal

I have written about some women's difficulties in leaving damaging relationships and the range of psychological effects that can flow from childhood experiences of sexual and emotional abuse. Over the past two decades, as women have given voice to their experience in general (in sexual relationships, in the family, the NHS, with education) the particular experiences of women, and subsequently men, who as children were sexually abused has forced our awareness of the extent of the problem, encouraging us to think about why this happens, what it means, why it is so widespread.

Sexual abuse is often less to do with sexuality than with the complex feelings of powerlessness, vulnerability, anger and longing intersecting with the defences of violence, projection and identification. Sexual aggression is the abusing adult's vehicle for the expression of distress. The abuser is involved in an antipathetic search for contact; an attempt to rid him or herself of psychic pain; the transmission of that pain to another; a way to force recognition on the other, to seek revenge for pain experienced and through the process of identification to squash the vulnerable self, seen in the other.

The abuser perceives in his or her 'prey' aspects of their own self that have been split off, repressed or denied. The other's naivety and 'innocence' jars, reminding the perpetrator of his or her own, once hurt, innocence. Through brutalising the 'innocent', one teaches it the lesson one learnt oneself and in the process reinforces the brutalisation of self.

Psychotherapy is often sought as a safe haven from abuse and is seen as the place to explore a history of being abused. Through it (and other routes) one is redefined as survivor. Until recently, psychoanalysis hid from itself an acknowledgement of the extent and frequency of sexual abuse, even at times refusing to hear accounts of abuse and interpreting them instead as imaginative desire. Today we are aware of sexual abuse within the therapeutic relationship itself.

Recent research in the United States, Holland and the United Kingdom has stated that 10 per cent of psychotherapists, psychologists and others who practise psychotherapy have engaged in sexual relations with past or present patients. This figure is in line with instances of abuse across the professions: 10 per cent of doctors, dentists, priests and lawyers are estimated to have sexual relations with their patients and clients.

These shocking statistics have a particular significance for the practice of psychotherapy. People seek psychotherapy only when they are vulnerable. Psychotherapy is not a recreational activity undertaken lightly but a healing relationship sought when the avenues of conventional social intercourse have failed to help people shift their distress. To find oneself sexually and emotionally exploited when in desperate need, not only compounds the problem but may make impossible a future positive relationship which can deal with past and present trauma.

The therapist who engages in sexual relations hijacks a client who is desperate to be understood, to make sense of their pain, to feel valued, noticed and regarded in a relationship so that she or he can then understand her or himself and reach a level of self-acceptance through internalising the authentic attention of another. The therapist's attention is misdirected, with extremely serious consequences.

Until recently only the lone voices of a few hurt individuals have dared to challenge the secrecy of the profession. Recently, an organisation POPAN (Prevention of Professional Abuse Network) has emerged to offer support through its monthly meetings to people who have experienced abuse within the therapy relationship.

Although individual professional bodies have a variety of methods of policing their own members, these institutions have been known to close ranks when a member has been accused of misconduct because they are concerned with upholding the reputation of their particular body. This makes them less than effective. Through the efforts of many individuals representing seventy diverse psychotherapy organisations under the able leadership of first Michael Pokorny (himself a psychiatrist, psychoanalyst and psychotherapist) and now Emmy van Deur-zen-Smith, the United Kingdom Council for Psychotherapy (UKCP) is establishing a voluntary registration of psychotherapists who are affiliated with one of the partnership organisations in the UK.

While membership of the register cannot guarantee the conduct of members, the registration board will develop powers to look into allegations of abuse, recommend therapeutic help for victims, deregister offenders and provide treatment for them. Unfortunately the Council has not dealt with one serious anomaly: psychotherapists of long standing or with foreign training who are unaffiliated to partnership organisations are absent from the register. The public may be misled into thinking that registration gives a therapist a clean bill of health, while absence from the register is suspect.

More useful perhaps is a body called SEPARATE (Sexual Ethics in Professional Relationships), which will make recommendations about the ethical issues at stake in therapeutic relationships. It will co-ordinate ethical standards between the various training bodies, make safety provisions for patients and develop treatment protocols for individual psychotherapists who find themselves in difficulty.

Because the therapy relationship is outside accustomed social norms, occurs in a one-to-one setting, necessarily implies a power imbalance, involves the possibility of intimacy and the working through of issues of trust and openness, the line between what is appropriate behaviour and what is inappropriate may confuse both patient and client. A leaflet which licensed psychotherapists in California are required to give clients at the beginning of treatment states boldly: *Sex is Always Wrong*. In New York State the registration body now obliges qualified clinicians who wish to keep their licences to take courses designed to increase their understanding of the psychological impact of sexual abuse.

These are the kinds of initiative being thought through here. SEPARATE and the UKCP are endeavouring, from the professional end, to find appropriate ways of protecting people who seek therapy. While I think these initiatives are crucial, I am still concerned about the lack of specific course content in most UK training programmes that address issues of gender, power and sexuality in the therapy relationship. Psychoanalytic theory and practice, while often drawing on case material of women, paradoxically still teaches psychological development as though it were masculine or gender-free, with perhaps six seminars in a four-year programme devoted to women. This continuing blind spot, this continuing difficulty of interrogating the meaning of gender in the individual's psyche, in the therapy relationship, its relation to sexuality, need, power, transference and countertransference must now be addressed seriously. This, in the end, along with the efforts of SEPARATE, will afford the public more reassurance that psychotherapists will not abuse the power invested in them by those who, when vulnerable, seek their help.

Between Parents and Children

The price we pay for the stiff upper lip is the stiff heart. And the stiff heart robs us of empathy. We are scared of children's needs and vulnerabilities because they remind us of our own which we have come to repress and fear.

The Stiff Heart

Several national and international conferences have focused on the conditions and policies that would enhance our capacity to create a culture which is more responsive to parents and children.

The psychotherapist hears a great deal about parenting gone wrong. But what makes it possible to be a good parent? Obviously parents need a level of economic and social stability. They need to be free of racist attacks. They need to be free of indiscriminate poverty, of war, of unemployment. These crucial factors affect our ability to parent well. But even if all the desirable economic and social factors are in place, we know only too well how impoverished some of our parenting skills are.

What is parenting? Parenting involves many processes: welcoming, caring, guiding, teaching, protecting, introducing the child into the family and the wider world. It means communicating values, ways of seeing, ways of thinking, ways of being. It means supporting children's activities and desires, containing

This article is based on a talk given for Exploring Parenthood in London in October 1992.

them, accepting their differences from us, tolerating what we find difficult. Above all it means respecting the child. But why should this be a problem?

The Children Act 1989 enshrines a set of values that have at their heart respect for the child. But this respect, this concern, contests what we see all around us. Children are exploited through child pornography, sexual abuse, violence and emotional neglect. The stories we hear about practices in some families, in children's homes and boarding schools should shock us because children have been placed in hazardous and unprotected environments. And it should make us think about what is making it possible for these abusive activities to occur.

What we find so very difficult, I suggest, is respecting children's emotional lives. The baby who cries inconsolably, the toddler whose mental and physical limits cause it immense frustration, the 9-year-old girl dealing with betrayal by an excluding coterie of girls, the teenager raging and sullen – all test our capacity for understanding and compassion. As parents, we witness emotional distress on a daily basis but we are ill equipped to respond to it. We may be scared of the pain or of the emotions our children show, feel that it demands action on our part and, not knowing what to do or how to respond, we may be tempted to silence it.

We find children's emotional lives difficult to respond to because we are habituated to ignoring, suppressing, disregarding our own. The price we pay as a culture for the stiff upper lip is the stiff heart. And the stiff heart not only makes us uncompassionate towards ourselves, it robs us of the capacity to respond empathically to those we wish to be open to. We are scared of children's vulnerabilities, children's needs, because they remind us of our own which in the course of our passage to adulthood we have come to repress and fear.

If we have repressed our emotional lives we not only become afraid of our children's needs to express theirs, we also become wary of vulnerability seeing it as a sign of weakness. We are scared of it and we have contempt for it.

We define adulthood by the way we manage our vulnerabilities and needs. Most often this means overriding them. We develop psychologies which have incorporated defences against the acceptance of personal vulnerability while over-developing our capacity to split off problematic or troublesome feelings. But responsible parenting requires precisely the opposite skills. It means becoming emotionally literate. Where now, by and large, we suffer with deeply impoverished emotional vocabularies, we need to direct the greatest effort towards re-educating ourselves, expanding our emotional vocabulary so that instead of designating feelings and vulnerabilities as fearful they are integrated into and inform our experience.

Disallowed feelings don't just conveniently slip away. On the contrary, being disregarded and having one's feelings ridiculed leads to bad feelings, difficult feelings, confused feelings which hang around – in distorted form – motivating many of our acts in ways that belie our capacity to be rational.

The boy whose fear of swimming is belittled continues to be afraid of the water. Ashamed and humiliated, he works hard to banish these fearful feelings. But unconsciously he remains fearful. He acts in counter-phobic ways, goading himself and his mates in the playground to overcome the scariest of activities. By the time he is an adult his capacity to tolerate fear has been converted into a complete contempt of anyone or anything fearful. He is unable to confront, experience and live through fear. When his child expresses fear, psychic alarm bells propel him to decry it, and the cycle turns.

Many parents say that they have never had the experience of being children, that they feel insufficiently grown up, and unprepared for the tasks of parenting. They feel they were forced to be responsible and grown up as children, and that now they feel fraudulent and unsure of themselves. What I think they are expressing is the gap between emotional and physical maturation. They are talking of a process in which from early on their emotional lives were not empathically responded to. In fact *they* learnt to cater to the emotional needs of those on whom they depended, rearranging their personal feelings in such a way as to not cause trouble. In the process they lost a part of themselves: the vulnerable part. So when they experience difficult emotional responses as adults they designate these as childish and suffer with self-contempt.

What's needed is to turn this equation upside down: to recognise that vulnerability and feelings are not only an important part of life, they are the building blocks of our own subjectivity and the basis for authentic interpersonal communication. Emotions are not a brake on rationality or action; they need to be understood and digested so that they can strengthen our practices and our policies.

As a culture we are terrified of emotions. We find them messy, arbitrary and difficult and, I should add, we count on women to mop them up. But responsible parenting requires the capacity to handle our children's feelings and to provide them with a safe environment in which their fears, their longings, their desires and their conflicts can be welcomed and tolerated. We need to provide this for our children as we simultaneously learn to provide it for ourselves.

The extent to which children's distress can be heard, lived through and passed on will depend on our capacity to become more emotionally literate ourselves. For teachers in our schools we need programmes directed at respecting children's emotional lives. Emotional illiteracy is at the bottom of many of the troubles children face in schools whether with learning, social relations of the playground, or between teachers and children.

In our maternity clinics we need lessons in the emotional impact of parenting, every bit as much as we need to learn parentcraft. Wherever parents collect we need to think of the ways in which public spaces can be opened up to provide a new discourse about parenting. We need businesses and state institutions to become more responsive themselves, to model – in their own parenting role – structures that are responsive and relational rather than arbitrary and cruel.

Children and parents are everywhere, and yet we act as

though children are still some sort of inconvenience. We need to stop the arbitrary disregard of both and offer structures of containment and support so that the vision and actuality of our future society embodies us as dignified whole people.

Lost Boys and Absent Fathers

Whether through separation, death or the constraints of long hours on the job, many children have the experience of absentee fathers.

Our cultural rules are being rewritten, and inserted into the new equation is the importance of the father, not merely as a symbolic, forbidding, distant and longed-for figure but as an active and engaged parent. Of course, many of us have been lucky to have fathers who enjoyed their children, played with them and introduced them to the world as well as modelling a masculinity that boys could emulate and girls appreciate.

But many more of us have known our fathers in a more elliptical way. He is a mainly mysterious figure, especially when we were young, when for short periods of time in the morning and possibly before bedtime, he entered the domestic zone bringing with him a particular atmosphere. Often our experience of him is mediated by our mother's view. She interprets his behaviour, prepares us for him, and vice versa. He may have been somewhat excluded from the domestic domain or he may have excluded himself, but on holidays and weekends he filled out the family and its ambience changed as his authority, his personality were accommodated.

But what of the child who grows up with a truly absent father? What happens to the child of the father who deserts his children; the father who for economic reasons works abroad or unsocial hours; the father who divorces and starts a new family, abandoning contact with the first; the father who dies; the father who was barely known by the mother?

And what especially happens to the sons who become the 'lost boys', bereft of the father–son relationship, trapped in the search for personal identity because of the difficulty of the relationship with a father who was either emotionally or physically absent.

The 'lost boys' represent three different experiences – death of the father, separation from the father, and an emotionally absent father – that between them encompass many boys' stories. The work of Robert Bly in his book about masculinity, *Iron John*, (whether we agree with it or not) attests to the hurt that so many men feel about the gaps in their relationships with their fathers. The phenomenon of men actively engaging in parenting and the ideological switch in which the baby appears harnessed to Dad in contemporary ads speak to the deep hurt, confusion, and wish to change what constitutes masculinity.

So what is so wrong with fathering as it is generally practised? What harm does it do to boys?

If father is physically and emotionally absent from the early life of the boy, whose formative experiences occur in a female-centred ambience (a setting in which the mother or her substitute(s) probably feels less supported than she might wish), his early internalisation will include the overwhelming image of the feminine. The emotional and physical nurture that provide for his growth will have come from a feminine source. The essence of the experience of self is imbued with the early merger and attachment to a woman. This would not be problematic if gender constraints in society did not impel at both an unconscious and conscious level a kind of relating that embodies notions of how masculinity must detach itself from the feminine in order to assert its difference (and historically its power).

From the mother's point of view, girls are felt to be the same, whereas boys are felt to be different. This experience of difference, in the absence of early positive opportunities to identify with sameness, causes boys, and later men, enormous difficulties at the very heart of their personalities. Their first most intimate and important relationship was with their mothers. Their experience of being recognised by another comes from a woman. Their first experience of contact is saturated with feminine identity, yet to achieve masculinity, as we currently understand it, the boy has to find a way of identifying with the masculine. Often this means he has to detach himself from this first attachment in order to reattach or identify with (heterosexual) masculinity.

Even if one accepts that this is an acceptable state of affairs, the problem arises because for many boys there is no available father to identify with. As the boy reaches out to attach himself to a man he often encounters an *absence* where he needs to find himself, and in that absence his relationship to his own masculinity is forged.

In so far as there is a real and active relationship, the boy can come to attach himself to the father. But if there is an absence, the boy is left severed from his attachment to the feminine while facing a vacuum where masculinity should be. This is compounded by the absence of male figures in the early environment in general, where nursery-school teachers, childminders, primary-school teachers and so on tend to be female.

The wrench from the maternal identification is a further problem because it is in the mother's ambience that the child has absorbed his first schooling in what constitutes relationship. His desires, hurts, longings, wants, anger, rages, disappointments, passions have all been experienced within his mother's ambit and authority. He has struggled with her, hated her and loved her. If bereft of another close relationship in which he can positively psychically align himself as he dis-identifies with the

113

feminine, then he will experience a double loss and a deep confusion about closeness: he will be confused about his relationship to the feminine, and at a loss about how to identify as a boy.

Often what we observe is the boy's (later the man's) need to repudiate the need for the feminine attachment, through a failure to admit to himself its importance. But what is also revealed is the 'hole' where the attachment to a father has not occurred. Masculinity is often held together by the boy's need to assert difference and to reassure himself, through the triumph of strength over vulnerability, that his disavowal of the feminine is valid, as though to acknowledge it would be to be overwhelmed by it.

The 'lost boy' becomes a father with an insecure sense of his own masculinity and a model of fathering that is no more than painting by numbers. His fears of vulnerability, of revealing that side of him, may propel him to stay away from active childrearing which would reawaken his early loss and confusions.

But it isn't only the sons who suffer. Fathers who lose their children or who have little access to them also lose the capacity to develop that crucial relationship; a relationship so often caricatured as framed by competitive and murderous struggles but a relationship which, if it occurs, allows the man access to his nurturing parts too. If the boy grows up with an active and engaged father his identification with masculinity can occur in conditions of security rather than in an implicit repudiation of the feminine.

The last two decades have opened the way for us to critique our reflexive parenting. Those who parent now have the chance to explore different models of parenting which, if heterosexual, could include both active mothers and fathers. We must ensure that our boys need not grow up to be lost.

Home Alone and Stigmatised

When it was first published, my article on absent fathers produced a hurt response from some single mothers, who read what I had to say as an attack on their situation. Although I was making a plea for men not to exclude themselves from parenting, I can quite see how that could have been experienced as an implicit critique of women who by choice or necessity are raising children on their own. I am deeply sorry about this.

Single mothering has always existed in contemporary society but it has been painted with different ideological brushstrokes which influence how we regard it. In truth, much of the parenting that goes on in the conventional nuclear family shares many features with single parenting in terms of the father's *actual* participation in childrearing. A father's physical presence in the home is often taken as evidence of active parenting even if he is rarely seen and rarely relates to his children. We normalise this practice while unconscionably denigrating women who choose to bring up children on their own.

For many women, the choice to parent alone stems from a desire to free themselves of the emotional bondage of an unsatisfactory adult relationship. Deciding to parent alone, the woman is under no illusion about her circumstances. Her longings and wishes to have a partner who also parents, who shares the pleasures, who recognises the emotional, educational and developmental needs of the child are not continually stimulated and disappointed. She is freer to devote her psychological and emotional energies to parenting.

During the Second World War, women bringing up children on their own were praised for their courage and saintliness. They were provided with reasonable support systems in terms of childcare and their social position was underpinned. Contrast this with similar women today whose failure or refusal to conform to the mythical heterosexual family with 2.2 children leads them to be blamed for the Newcastle riots, the rebellion in Los Angeles, crime, drugs and all manner of social problems.

At the heart of the present critique of single mothers lies the issue of intentionality. Swathes of moral critiques envelop women who dare to declare their right to have children on their own. Pregnant 16-year-olds do it 'to get housing and love' while single working women are disparaged and their babies contemptuously described as the latest 'designer toys'. Among those who attack the hardest are men who have been deprived of active fathers themselves; they then turn this loss into rage at unknown women who have the nerve to recognise the unbalanced nature of many parenting arrangements by making a positive decision to parent alone.

Paradoxically, women who *have* to parent on their own through bereavement, divorce or a partner's work absence are offered sympathy. If one can cast the woman and her child or children as victims then they become palatable. We feel sorry for her. We feel sorry for them. We regard her efforts as valiant. We sympathise with her difficulties, selflessness, isolation and economic hardship. We might make that little bit of extra effort with her children. But a woman who makes a positive decision to parent on her own is besmirched.

In trying to understand the emotional force of the venom

poured on women who do parent on their own and to try – in so far as that is possible – to separate it from the weight of ideology that encourages us to fit our emotional responses into a set of moralisms, it strikes me that there are three main issues at work which serve to undermine single mothers.

First, single mothers force us to recognise a woman's independence, capability and power. Her labour – both the emotional and domestic labour implied in raising a child alone – is no longer concealed behind the veil of partnership. Just consider for a moment a man who is widowed or whose partner leaves him with the children. His ability to manage this task (which is considerable for anyone) is considered herculean. What is usually exploited is now seen. And so we ask: is the accomplishment of single mothers less herculean than the accomplishment of single fathers? If we fail to judge single mothers as quasi-immoral, if we desist from patronising them, then their accomplishment becomes visible. If they are visible we have to recast them as strong, able, powerful.

Secondly, in the ironic twist so characteristic of the intersection of morality and problematic feelings, the difficulties I was writing about in relation to men's frequent absence as parents are loaded on to a criticism of women. Women become the recipients of the rage, hurt and distress about a father's neglect of his family. The anger is projected on to single mothers and they are blamed for causing paternal absence. All single mothers – those who are single by choice or those who are abandoned – become a vehicle for the boy's, and later the man's, fury at the loss of his father. The psyche attacks the person who was there, generalises the attack to other women, and then finds some explanation in moral platitudes for its pain.

Men's rage in this area is linked to all of our complex feelings towards our mothers. When mothers are the primary caregivers and nurturers they become extremely powerful in all of our psyches. They have the capacity to make us feel soothed, held, contained and cared for. But when in their emotional orbit we feel fragmented, confused, hurt or angry, we feel a great need

117

for them to put us back together again. This dependency on the mother and the relative lack of power of the child, coupled with a situation where the mother may be desperately unsupported herself, can lead to an unconscious rage at 'mothers' for the pain that has been felt but not digested.

But it is not only men, of course, who moralise or who feel threatened by women who choose to become single parents. For women locked in unsatisfactory relationships, the single mother represents freedom and a way out. But this freedom can feel frightening if one's sense of security is caught up in an unsatisfactory attachment. Fear and the feeling of being trapped combine to create their own form of moralising. By designating what is different and outside as bad, one can relieve oneself (temporarily) of the difficulty of facing the pain that one's own circumstances are generating. Fear and uncertainty fuel the need to distance the self from alternatives.

In writing about single mothers, I do not mean to undercut my remarks about the difficulties that can face boys growing up in families where fathers are (emotionally) absent. To illuminate psychic processes, as I did in that article, is quite a different matter from using superficial psychological argument to bolster contentious moralistic polemic. Moralism and feelings are often collapsed together in the attempt to give more force to a spurious argument, but deep psychological understanding leads to the ability to tolerate difficulties and differences rather than to exclude them by false moralism.

Why a Half-Nelson is So Gripping

Wrestling is big business. Wrestling stars rival movie stars in the salaries they earn, fan clubs abound, worshipful armies of (mainly) boys and men watch wrestling weekly, buy magazines and memorabilia, discuss the moves, and buy expensive tickets to wrestling extravaganzas within an hour or two of them being on sale.

Last month the World Wrestling Federation's (WWF) Summer Slam came to Wembley Stadium and 80,000 fans, plus me, attended. It was an amazing sight to observe and be part of and it set me thinking about what and why this is such a massive attraction.

Like a rock concert, where you can hardly hear, so at a wrestling match, even in press seats, you can hardly see. In fact the only way to see is to watch the TV monitor – kindly supplied by the Stadium for the press – because the large video screen doesn't produce a good image until sunset so for most of the match it is useless. Watching the monitor gives you pretty much the same impression as watching on TV at home except for the helpful fact that you are with 80,000 enthusiasts and the unhelpful fact that if you are not a Wembley aficionado, you are freezing.

119

But there is a lot to see. The costumes are fantastic and imaginative. Some of the wrestlers and their sidekick managers wear elaborate make-up. There are spotlights and tracking lights. Music brings the wrestlers on and off the set, creating a whole extravaganza more akin to the Oscar ceremonies than what one might imagine goes on at a wrestling match. The evening, which lasted four hours – although fans arrived a good three hours beforehand – is divided up into about nine different fights. Audience participation through vocalisation is intense and an important part of the show. There are good guys and bad guys. Preeners and ugly guys. Each fight is like a playlet telling a reasonably predictable story; operatic in its use of drama and balletic in its movement, the scene around the ring becomes quite compelling.

At one level, an assessment of what accounts for the appeal of wrestling might include an understanding of the identification the child or adult makes with the fight, with children in particular having the opportunity to experience, without censure, their feelings of love and hate. Or there can be identification with the wrestler's personality. Or one could argue that enjoying wrestling, practising the moves, being caught up with the wrestlers is a way to feel strong and invincible when inside oneself one feels the opposite. These facets of the matches are probably accurate up to a point but I was struck by other aspects of the extravaganza that may explain some of the special appeal and hold that WWF wrestling (and its competitor WCW, World Championship Wrestling) has on so many boys (and quite a few girls) aged 7 and up.

First – and this seems unique to wrestling – is what goes on at the borders of the wrestling ring itself. There is considerable activity on the periphery of the ring which involves not only the official wrestlers but their henchmen and, at Summer Slam, henchwomen. These characters come in, bare-arsed to disarm the competition, or bearing weapons. This apparent 'breaking of rules' suggests some vicarious excitement with the fracturing of boundaries. The impermissible is flagrantly displayed. The wrestling ring is one arena in which strength is contested, but the boundary, which represents the place of arbitrariness on the one hand and containment on the other, is where much of the contest takes place. It is the capacity to play with this boundary too, to dare to breach it, that holds psychological importance. Psychological development requires absorbing, understanding and testing the rules, feeling safe in the knowledge that they can't be broken too much and titillated by others' transgressions. WWF and WCW allow kids (and grown-ups) to enter into this territory and experience larger-than-life figures breaking the rules that we feel so continually tied by. That's thrilling and fascinating.

Another aspect of the appeal of wrestling is the fact that the kids do seem to be quite clear that the fighting isn't for real. The ability to distinguish between pretend and real, which is an important developmental step for all of us, is continually transgressed as the wrestling spectator becomes engrossed in the activity in and around the ring. Wrestling is theatre and the suspension of disbelief is interesting, I think, because many psychoanalysts theorise that it is the boundary between fantasy and reality that provides the site of our capacity for imagination and creativity. So although, on the face of it, to become passionately involved in the outcome of a predetermined result seems odd, one is actually doing more than that. We are creating out of our imaginative sense the result, just as in babyhood we imagine that we create the breast, the parent, the bear that magically appears. As in all imaginative acts, we feel a certain potency and aliveness. While parents may despair that their children are caught up in what seems a very passive activity, in fact important imaginative psychological processes to do with fantasy and reality are actively engaging them.

I was also intrigued by the outcome of the various acts. Each fight features WWF favourites dancing about on stage, bouncing one another around until for no obvious reason one is declared the winner. That is one of the most striking parts of the evening for me. It really was not clear why any particular individual or team should win. No superior strength or skill is displayed by one side or the other and apart from the obvious psychological point of having the only British wrestler – The British Bulldog – win on British soil, the outcome of the other matches was a mystery until declared. In other sports where the outcome is also unclear the skill of the players makes it hard to guess a result. But in a sport where the contest is a set-up from the start – and the kids know that – it was a surprise to watch so many acts in which the same unpredictability of outcome could be observed.

So I wonder whether this unpredictability might be intrinsic to aspects of wrestling's psychological appeal. The thought that anyone can be a winner brings a certain feeling of relief and rationality to kids whose world is so invidiously, capriciously and incomprehensibly competitive. If winning is the name of the game, then not simply identifying with one's heroes or villains but realising that there is nothing intrinsically brilliant about them may be comforting. All is really equal and it is simply chance that does or doesn't single one out. If we try to enter the child's world, we can see that this might be a satisfactory solution to the inequities children experience but have little conceptual framework for. Some win, some lose but there is no significant difference between competitors.

My final observation relates to the proclamations of greatness on the part of the individual wrestlers. This is an important part of their gestalt, much as it was for Muhammed Ali but in a much more exaggerated sense. In the dressing-rooms, in interviews before and after the match, they declare their superiority without humility. This bragging is extremely attractive to kids who are absorbing the idea that self-promotion is distasteful, inappropriate and unwelcome. But the thing about kids is that they do have moments of feeling great about what they can achieve today that they didn't manage yesterday, that they are on a growing curve in which they are constantly changing and getting to know new bits of themselves. The wrestlers' hyped-up pride speaks to them in a private part of themselves which would like to be admired, to be able to say, 'I'm Great', but which often instead gets punished for 'showing off'.

The wrestlers are essentially show-offs who break the rules, get away with it and are adored. It is the other side of the heroic rescuer prince that captivates different parts of boys' imaginative sense. It is certainly not pretty to watch if you dislike violence or macho activity and are in the least bit gender conscious. But it certainly sets you thinking if you live with a child enamoured of wrestling.

Why Girls Can Be So Ghastly To One Another

'My 13-year-old daughter suffers terribly from the cattiness and nastiness of some of her so-called friends. I've noticed how cruel girls can be, especially compared to boys who seem to fight much more cleanly.'

We may remember only too well from our own experience the cruelty and heartache that can exist in girls' relationships with one another. While it is particularly prevalent among pre-adolescents, this phenomenon can start in nursery school and continue well on into adult life, where treacherous behaviour between women has given rise to the appellation 'bitch'.

Margaret Atwood writes poignantly about girlhood cruelty in her novel *Cat's Eye*. The adult protagonist, a successful artist, finally feels strong enough in herself to re-encounter the relationships that so scarred her. Betrayal by a woman in adult life is a source of sorrow and distress. But although one may feel defenceless in the face of this, there *are* ways to overcome the hurt and to avoid repeated injury. In childhood, however, the consequences of cruelty are more serious. They may mean one is ostracised from a friendship network, that one is picked on or ganged up against, that one's childhood friendships are unstable. In more worrying cases it may mean one experiences so much bullying that one dreads going to school and dreads the journey home where cruelty is enacted well away from the eyes of adults. One may even contemplate suicide.

In the course of my work as a psychotherapist I not only hear about the hurt women have experienced as victims of other children's cruelty or as agents of cruelty themselves, but I hear about the pain parents feel when they observe their daughters caught up in exclusionary games or hurtful behaviours that seem hard to unravel. Vendettas can occur in which an excluded child finds it hard to reintegrate herself into any grouping so remains dolefully on the outside.

A more common scenario involves shifting allegiances whereby fidelity is sworn one day and broken the next. Laura and Georgia are best friends. A new girl, Annabel, joins the class and Laura feels drawn to her. Georgia feels threatened by the new girl's presence. Meanwhile Annabel wants to be Laura's friend but she doesn't want to be Georgia's. She courts Laura and they become good friends. Laura wants all three of them to be friends but instead Laura and Annabel begin to gang up on Georgia. Laura feels bad about it but does it because it seems to be the price of the friendship with Annabel, who interests her. In time Annabel gets fed up with Laura and starts a friendship with Carol, who was getting close to Georgia. Laura goes back to Georgia to make amends, but just as that happens, Annabel tries to bust in again and sweet-talk Laura, and so on.

The point of this story is not to follow the ins and outs of who is excluding whom, and who is making alliances with whom, but to observe the volatility, passion and hurt that accompany all these shifting allegiances. Georgia finds no solace from her mother's comments that anyone who treats her that way is no friend. Meanwhile Laura feels guilty for betraying Georgia and Annabel is clearly a distressed child who is driven to fracture existing relationships.

These three girls are caught up in a phenomenon in which

insecurity and hurt drive the relationships. Why is it that girls' relationships can be such a seesaw? And is there any way to help girls suffer less?

Girls are raised with the social injunction to be caring, thoughtful and to put everyone else first. Their identity will be formed not through their differences from one another but through relational capacities – to identify, empathise and tune in to others' experience. Frequently discouraged from taking the initiative unless it is in relational terms and in regard to the meeting of others' needs, little girls can feel bereft of a forum that gives them recognition in their own right. Deprived of recognition, one's identity becomes confirmed in sameness and similarity, through making relationships which mirror aspects of the self.

In this they are unlike their brothers, whose gender difference from their mothers brought both difference and closeness into their very first close relationship and for whom difference in general is a central aspect of self and the establishment of a personal identity, whether outside the family or in their peer group; a girl's identity is confirmed in sameness and similarity. Difference is a more problematic state; it goes against the emotional grain. Self-identity is more commonly found through matching oneself to the needs of someone else and then finding oneself in that identification. Thus friendships become import-ant stepping stones on the road to finding an identity. Bonding closely and finding a best friend with whom they can bare their soul solves some of the problems of recognition.

But at the same time as close bonding provides a form of recognition and of course the pleasure that sharing mutual interests brings, closeness can also feel both precarious and cloying. These two aspects of young girls' friendships conspire to make problems.

In friendships between girls, the closeness comes from a sense of knowing the other, of feeling understood, of being able to stand in the other's shoes and imagine her experience. In this fantasy (because after all we can only ever imagine that we know what another is thinking and feeling), girls project all their own desires and need for connection and caring that they have habitually lavished on others. They seek in friendships with one another that same attention for themselves and unconsciously hope that their most secret desires will be recognised and met. But this closeness can be cloying because it isn't accurate, because it depends upon so much projection and fantasy and because the bonding relies on the denial of difference. This impossible state of affairs leads to painful disruption when conformity is no longer possible. The disharmonious party is excluded (or excludes herself) in favour of another or a group of others who will deny difference as the price of closeness.

So what our girls need is the encouragement to risk being different, to bond on a basis which allows similarity and difference rather than enforcing the suppression of differences which will inevitably explode and threaten the friendship. And they also need help with feelings of abandonment, for such feelings are at the root of the need to bond so intensively and to disavow one another so intently. Abandonment feelings aren't solved by superglued friendships. They are temporarily eased. When feelings of abandonment are aroused, 'cattiness' and meanness are employed as ways to fend off the threat.

The more we allow girls to find an identity that recognises rather than exploits their personal needs, the less compelling will be their need to fasten on to the chosen one in friendship while simultaneously brutally excluding the other.

Look Honey, the Perfect Kid

One of the difficulties leading to continual tension and disharmony between children and parents arises when children turn out to be very different from the expectations, fantasies and imaginings of their parents.

Brenda was the second child of academic parents. In contrast to her older sister who had read law, at the age of 25 Brenda had not really fastened on anything that interested her. Her life seemed to drift aimlessly and she was vaguely depressed. Although she rejected 'success' and materialism, the odd jobs she found often left her in financial need. She would then turn to her parents for help. This irritated and worried them.

Her father was forever sitting her down to encourage her to make plans; her mother gave her instructions about how to live her life. Brenda was resentful of her parents' overtures; she felt as though she was always disappointing them and failing them.

Meanwhile, each parent suffered privately. Not only did they blame themselves but they blamed each other, imagining that if only the other would pull their weight, in some magical way the situation would be straightened out. Every time there was a crisis with Brenda, tension ensued between the parents. The father would scold the mother for worrying and put forward some intellectual argument for understanding the rightness of Brenda's development. The mother would feel flattened, feel that her worries were being trivialised and that she was being portrayed as a rejecting mother and an ambitious bitch.

This kind of scenario, in which parents become estranged from one another in dealing with the perceived problems of their children, is often exacerbated by each parent's feelings of grief and disappointment about their children. If these cannot be shared then recrimination (either self-directed or directed at one's partner) becomes the mode of relating. What Brenda's parents needed was a chance to share their upset about Brenda with one another. They needed to mourn for their fantasies about who Brenda was meant to be for them, as a couple and as individuals, so that they could stop foisting their disappointment on to her and each other.

Finding a way to share these painful feelings with one another enabled them to examine the unvoiced expectations they had. Her mother realised that she had wanted Brenda's life to be purposeful. She didn't want Brenda to suffer as she had in coming to take her working life and purpose seriously. Brenda's mother had been embattled with her parents about having a career in the first place, and had wanted to offer her daughter a smooth pathway to self-expression.

Her husband recognised that he liked having a daughter who continued to need him; that he had an interest in her dependency. He had been unsupported as a child and had longed for parental protection. In being at the ready when Brenda needed him, he felt wanted and valued. His own work trajectory had included a period of dropping out in his twenties before he became a successful composer. He worried that Brenda was unhappy but he didn't fear for her future for he had found himself rather late.

As Brenda's parents recognised their pain, then the roots of some of the expectations they had held for Brenda, they were able to join together to provide useful support for her. They realised that she was indeed very different from them and that her personal choices were ones they didn't really understand; that they needed to disengage, to stop interfering and let her get on with her life. If they were going to offer financial support they saw that they needed to do this without lectures, strings or planning sessions about how Brenda was managing her finances. The parents' ability to act together allowed Brenda in turn to separate from them. Where her choices had been made as an act of rebellion but also as an unconscious indictment of her parents for what they had and hadn't provided, she was now able to think more clearly about her circumstances and her life. Since she no longer felt she had to refer to them, to seek approval or disapproval, she could face her own depression and try to understand and shift it.

Many parents find it extremely difficult not to enter the emotional space of their children and not to feel alarmed by their children's differences. We enter parenting with expectations we are unaware of. Even though we may be conscious that we do not want to reproduce our own childhoods and our parents' attitudes towards us, this doesn't prevent us from becoming anxious about our children's development.

When our children turn out to make choices other than those we might have wished, when they show inclinations that confuse us, when their interests contradict or stand beyond our comprehension, we may suffer private agonies because of our unconscious expectations. If these agonies cannot be recognised they may get diverted into anxiety, which is then dumped on to the child, making him or her the bearer of parental anxiety and creating feelings in them that what they are about is somehow wrong.

Parenting inevitably throws up a wish that our children will express aspects of ourselves that we have not been able to realise, and that our children will be able to enter life without having to learn for themselves all the painful lessons we have suffered. These wishes combine with another important feature of parenting: the wish to undo our own childhood hurts. This hoped-for reparative aspect of parenting can go seriously askew if the parent is also judgemental, even if in different ways to their own parents.

Parents can discover that they have reproduced rather than having transformed the parenting they have experienced. A husband's bitter comment that his wife is just like her mother can be deeply wounding for it fails to help her to come to grips with what is compelling her to act in ways she would rather not act. But the shift needs to happen within the couple, not simply within the individual.

Joan and Carol, two women parenting together, noticed that one of them became overprotective towards their 13-year-old son, while the other seemed almost lackadaisical. This polarisation not only confused the child, who found it hard to develop a sense of appropriate caution, but it left both parents isolated, angry and feeling misunderstood. As they tried to change the dynamic between them, they realised that they both had to take responsibility for expressing their fears about their son's safety.

As it became possible for Joan and Carol to share their concerns with one another, they could work through their rational and irrational fears without defensively needing to deny each other's position. They had manoeuvred themselves into a corner in which each of them had been defending a position, but when Joan's propensity for caution had been recognised and owned by Carol, Joan's wish to give their son as much freedom as was realistic could be articulated and together they could make that a possibility.

Parental differences are often polarised where a more accurate state of affairs would be the recognition that inner conflict becomes conveniently divided between two people. This division, rather than helping the child, or the parents individaully or as parents, leaves everyone isolated and disgruntled. When we add to this the unconscious expectations placed on children, the parent – child relationship can become fraught. In recognising that there are projections and disappointments, and that mixed feelings characterise much of parenting, it is possible to begin to see children as separate individuals to whom one has responsibilities, rather than as creations who exist to match parental desire.

Sibling Rivalry

One tried to throw his down the toilet; another cut off one side of his hair; yet another set fire to her room. Cruelty towards a sibling often occurs in early childhood. The shocked parent, witnessing the glee with which a first-born torments a brother or sister, may recoil from the situation, scold the child or absent her or himself hoping somehow that what they saw wasn't really going on and didn't truly reflect sweet Emma's feelings about Dan.

But sibling rivalry is a pervasive phenomenon that can dog a person through adult life, not only affecting their relationship with their brothers and sisters, but influencing how they respond to colleagues and friends and their own children.

As family size decreases and children's entry into the world becomes spaced, many first-born children live through an experience of receiving a considerable amount of intense attention for several years. With the birth of a sibling, attention has to be shared and there is quite a dramatic loss for the first-born. Often this loss goes unacknowledged and in its place they are given the role of 'little helper' or the 'bigger one', now expected to be able to do all kinds of things for themselves or by themselves.

This transformation from being the baby to being the older one has, to be sure, advantages, but often the disadvantages, the rapid change in position, the loss of attention are neglected.

Most parents remind themselves of the rationale for extending their family. They remember how Emma expressed great desire to have a sister or brother; of how they wanted a companion in the family for their child; of how much they had wanted a brother or sister when they were little; of how much they enjoy their adult relationship with their sibling.

Rationales such as these, which are of course completely valid, can nevertheless have the effect of diverting our attention from what is required when siblings are having a difficult time with one another. If we can help children cope with the negative aspects of their experience of having a sibling then the harmony and co-operation which is so often missing in family life has a fairer chance of occurring.

For the first-born, especially, the arrival of a baby is frequently felt as a displacement, a punishment and a loss. As the older child (or older children) sees the baby fussed over, hears the constant stream of phone calls and watches visitors cooing over the new-born; as she or he is expected to accede assent to the rhetorical question for the hundredth time, 'How do you like your baby brother/sister, isn't he/she so cute', and fields uncomfortable comments such as 'Aren't you lucky to have such a lovely new sister/brother', or, 'Mummy and Daddy loved you so much they wanted to have another one of you', the child may feel a mixture of guilt and resentment. No, it doesn't think this cry baby is at all cute. No, it doesn't feel itself to be lucky in the least bit. Get this baby away. Get rid of it. And if you don't I will, or I will make its life or your life torture.

This attitude can give way to a child's wondering why, if it was so very much loved, another child was brought in. After all Mummy loves Daddy and Daddy loves Mummy but they don't go bringing in extra Mummies and Daddies. And, of course, if the child has felt insecure before the arrival of the newcomer, the new baby becomes a ready-made explanation for why they feel insufficiently loved.

As they grow up, the tensions and insecurities get re-expressed. The older children may protect the younger at the same time as they find ways to trip them up. Siblings may enjoy one another and may in adult life have lots in common. However, many adult siblings can go in and out of war with one another; feel overcome by a competitiveness, or find it hard to shift the patterns of relating they established in childhood. Cathy was never allowed to win an argument against her older sister Janet because she her mother said: 'was so much more intelligent she mustn't show her sister Janet up'.

Today Cathy feels impelled to protect her sister and older women colleagues at work from her own competence. She feels uneasy about her own success at work and undermines herself. She makes decisions that feel correct but then she mistrusts her judgement. This hiding of her capabilities first from Janet and now from herself involves her in a tortuous muddle of undoing her initiatives or at the very best doubting them. Janet, meanwhile, the pretty and kind one finds it hard to feel her own considerable competence. She unconsciously and habitually projects on to Cathy her own strengths, not being able to shake the limited view of herself as the 'pretty and kind one'. Both Cathy and Janet look to other woman-to-woman relationships that will allow them to challenge these restricted views of self. They are anxious to be seen with a range of capabilities and attributes, but are often so caught up in projecting the image of self that they were given in relation to one another that they find it almost impossible to incorporate traits that were given to the other.

The dividing up of attributes between children in an attempt to encapsulate their individuality – 'Jake's athletic and brilliant, Sara mathematical and beautiful and Ben musical and dreamy' – can have the effect of imprisoning the individual in an identity that, while it doesn't fit, is taken on lest they be rejected. So Jake despite his interest in music has become accustomed to concealing this, leaving the field for his younger brother. Meanwhile he feels burdened by the need to continue to prove his brilliance at 34. Seen as brilliant, he can't imagine what it would be like to give up that identity even though it constrains him.

Along with a tendency to divide children's personalities is another problematic notion: that of treating each one in exactly the same way. To avoid squabbles at the dinner table or the sweet shop, each child receives the same amount of goodies because it is 'fair'. Fair it might be, but this response bypasses each individual's need or desire and substitutes a concept of fairness where what might be more helpful would be to address the feelings of jealousy and competition that many a child feels towards a sibling.

What needs recognising and responding to is not equal shares of time or tangerines, but attention to the emotional states of the individual children. We need to feel ourselves into our children's experiences – to see what might be going on from their point of view. To see that a first-born needs a chance to pour out the feelings of loss, of abandonment, even of betrayal that he or she feels towards a parent for displacing them. Their hurt, however difficult for the parent to bear, needs to be acknowledged and heard. Similarly, the 'baby' in the family may need a parent's help to get out from under that identity and have its own initiatives valued; a middle child to find a way to be special, and so on. If parents can respond to the child's perceived hurts then the child may be able to free itself from constantly reiterating its position in the family and the felt precariousness of it.

Sibling relationships often feel desperately stuck in rivalry and competitiveness. Recognising the insecurity each can feel, and acknowledging each's individual needs, is an important step, enabling the child to feel valued for her or himself.

Don't Eat That: You'll Spoil Your Appetite

A preoccupation with food, fatness, thinness and fitness continues to pervade our culture. At any given time more than 80 per cent of women are depriving themselves of food in one way or another. There is scarcely a woman between the ages of 20 and 50 who doesn't wish that some part of her body was different. Aerobics classes, fitness gymnasiums and the running track are full of women and men 'working out'.

While these activities may sound relatively benign, for many the attempt to reshape bodies and limit appetites stems from the hope that conflicts, unmet desire, inconvenient emotional or physical appetites can be assuaged through control of the body. What certainly is not benign is the impact this socially sanctioned obsession has on our children's eating and their attitudes towards their bodies.

A staggering 70 per cent of 9-year-old girls in San Francisco are dieting because although the majority of them are scrawny, they *think* they are too fat and they believe they must curb their appetites. Although British research figures are lower they can't, I fear, conceal a similarly worrying picture here. Certainly the incidence of serious eating problems – anorexia and bulimia

139

– are on the rise in younger and younger populations. Body preoccupations are now reaching in and stealing the childhoods of our young ones.

So how are we as parents, role models, teachers etc. unwittingly contributing to this problem? Often grown-ups battle with children over food. There are substantial reasons, of course. Providing a nourishing diet for children at a time when so much doubt has been cast on the safety of our food is not a trivial issue. The ever-changing nutritional advice we are offered adds to the confusion. Twenty years ago steak, eggs, cheese and milk were considered nutritious foods. Today we learn that they can harm us, that we need to take care that we don't eat too much cholesterol, that we shouldn't lay down fat cells that will never go away, that we should avoid tartrazine and additives, dairy products and polyunsaturates.

Parents want to introduce their children to wholesome foods in such a way that the appeal of franchised fast food is lessened, that it is not a treat or something to lust for, but a type of food occasionally enjoyed. But in achieving this delicate balance they need help in sorting through the psychological and nutritional minefield that surrounds them on all sides.

We find ourselves being inconsistent. We imagine that we know our children's appetites better than they do. One moment we bid them wait – 'Don't eat that: you'll spoil your appetite' – the next we urge them to override the personal signals that tell them whether they are hungry or not, and bid them eat: 'You can't go to school on an empty stomach.' We can veer between letting them choose what they like to eat and panicking that what they choose will not be good for them. We worry if they are picky eaters and praise them if they are good eaters. We equate food with nurture, we equate food with caring. And when they refuse our offerings we can feel dashed and rejected.

Many factors contribute to parents' confusion about the whole area of children and food. Parenting is a skill we learn on the job and for which we are underprepared and we can feel insecure in so many of its aspects. Barely out of the womb for a minute, the baby is put to the breast, which provides it with warmth, physical welcome, succour and nourishment. We worry about whether we are doing it right, if the baby is getting enough, if we are giving enough, if we are winding the baby properly. Insecurity and concern pervade the early relationship, and difficulties we encounter in those interactions can set up an emotional ambience that causes trouble to mother and child alike.

Our *own* difficulties concerning food are bound to spill over into our relationship with children. If we have become fearful of our own eating we may be afraid to let our children discover food preferences, food ambiences, ways of eating that please them. We may find it hard to believe that they can select foods that are right for them and that are healthy. We may feel tempted not to introduce certain foods in the false hope that they will never crave them. We may be so distanced from our own mechanisms of satisfaction and satiety that we interrupt their discovery of their own.

But if we observe our children we may marvel at their relaxed attitude towards food, their ability to stop in the middle of a mouthful of chocolate, to leave ice-cream behind in the dish. In short, their inbuilt undistorted relationship to appetite. If we can refrain from meddling too much, if we can distinguish between our children's needs and our own they have a chance to have a different relationship to food. They will learn that physiological hunger requires food. That emotional problems require emotional solutions.

The problems we have with food are linked to the insecurities we have about our bodies. Many a parent regularly wishes that her or his body were a different shape or size. Many a parent disparages his own appearance when confronted with a mirror. Many a parent is unable to get dressed without making a negative comment about herself. Many a parent is so distant from a feeling of comfort with her body from the *inside* that she has to assess it from the *outside* before she knows how she feels.

The adult's alienation, shame and disgust, and wish to mould the body into a more perfect form, make it hard for the parent to convey a sense that the body, the physical manifestation of selfhood, is stable and safe. Parents may feel and express tremendous delight in the beautiful body of their baby, toddler, pre-adolescent or adolescent child. But the parents' delight will be received by the child in adulterated form. It is tinged with the knowledge the child has perceived of the parents' insecure relation to their bodies. A sense of precariousness follows: 'How long will my body be acceptable?' 'What must I do to maintain its acceptability?' The child learns that its body, its physical abode, is not inviolate.

The body insecurity we experience as adults is unwittingly passed on to our children. The child lives in a body that is constantly changing as it matures. The child has to adjust to and cope with these changes while facing the daunting psychological task of absorbing confusing parental messages about bodies. And so the circle turns. The corporeally uncertain child becomes the corporeally uncertain adolescent. The corporeally uncertain adolescent becomes the corporeally uncertain adult who – despite the best of intentions – becomes the uncertain parent who breeds body insecurity into their offspring, making them prey for the vultures of the fashion and diet industries.

But we can intervene. We can observe and challenge our reflexive attitudes towards our bodies and our appetites and our children's bodies and their appetites. As we understand the ways in which we unconsciously undermine our children in relation to their appetites, how we give them mixed messages, we can begin to reverse the process. We can create a food environment for our children that encourages them to trust their appetites from the inside. We can try to convey to them unambiguously that their bodies are a safe place in which to live. We owe them their birthright: to grow up unafraid of their appetites and proud of their bodies.

Starting School

For many of us, long out of school, the rhythm of the year still starts in September. More profoundly than its calendar counterpart, an Indian summer or an autumnal chill signifies beginnings. For some this is an exciting time. There is promise and hope – a welcome feeling of getting stuck into projects, work, enterprises or learning that is inviting. For others though it's an unnameable dread; a sense of foreboding, of time closing in. Fear. Depression.

September melancholia may well be something one lives with without much awareness that the gloom and despondency are cyclical. Although cognizance in itself doesn't relieve symptoms, by naming, recognising and anticipating them, it can make such symptoms easier to live with. And if the meanings attached to symptoms can be excavated, the symptoms themselves may shift.

The despondency and claustrophobia felt by those who sink in September can often be traced back to difficult experiences in starting school for the first time and it is those that I shall be addressing here. But it is also the case that the hope and anticipation of good experience during one's schooling can be suddenly erased by a bad autumn term, the memory of which gets expunged from consciousness but repeats itself in an unarticulated worry every adult September.

This is one of the few Western countries that in certain quarters still holds in high esteem the belief that sending children away from home at an early age is good for their education, good for building character, good for their development, good for the family and good for society. Although the vast majority of the population do not send children to boarding schools (for economic or ideological reasons), the fact that the Royals, most cabinet ministers and senior civil servants were educated and educate their children in this way, disproportionately influences us as a society. Childhood and schooling thus cast are an introduction to life in which premature separation from the ambience of home, learning how to cope silently with loss, confusion, bad food, constant regimentation, ranking and bullying are the norm. And this cruelty, this attitude towards schooling and towards children filters through into both the private and the state education sectors, influencing how children are introduced to school and to the classroom, and influencing what is taught there and how it is taught.

The intersection between public policy and the emotional climate of a school is intricate. At a time in which the importance of the three Rs, discipline and uniforms is stressed, to divert attention from cost-cutting, creative supportive learning would mean that teachers were not attacked by their Education Secretary, heads would not be obsessed with the bottom line, pupils would not be terrorised by the need to make high scores. The individual school atmosphere may or may not be warm, accommodating, inviting and accepting. It may welcome children's individuality and accept the nervousness and apprehension that little ones approaching school for the first time experience. But more often, especially now, it does not.

Many teachers, overstretched by the non-teaching aspects of their jobs and by the many social problems that devolve on to schools, encouraged to think in terms of testing, frustrated by

144

the lack of opportunity to put into practice their gifts and skills, still try to make a safe and exciting environment for their classes. But they may have little space to handle the reluctant child who is fearful of school. The teacher may have had no courses on what to do about the handful of children who cling monkey-like to their parents at the schoolroom door in the morning wailing not to be put down. They are unable to intervene to help the child, to help the parent help the child and to ease the situation for themselves in the classroom.

And the situation, while not insurmountable, is indeed rich in difficult feelings. For the parent, unpeeling and leaving a screaming child at school is deeply distressing. There is grief at having to say goodbye to a little 4-year-old in tears, there is much worry that our tender baby will be all right, and painful feelings of separation *for the parent* as well as the child. We feel embarrassment that our child is not handling the morning separation as 'maturely' as his or her cohort. Whether this is a first, second, third, fourth or fifth child, there will be poignancy at this marker of 'independence'. It means the end of a particular kind of relationship for the parent. The child is 'handed over' for six hours a day to someone who may have thirty other little babes in their care. School is a big step from nursery, childmind ing or play group, and a parent may have considerable sorrow in letting go. They may also feel relief, pride and pleasure in their child's new adventure.

The child may pick up the parent's feelings of loss, anxiety and excitement, and may feel impelled to handle the transition to school well for the sake of the parent. Children may be muted in the expression of their reactions because they are so aware of their parents' emotional state and know somewhere that their safety depends upon keeping their Mum, Dad or Nan as unanxious as possible.

This is one scenario and a far from uncommon one. It is reinforced by an attitude that says, 'Don't make a fuss', 'There is nothing to worry about', 'Keep a stiff upper lip'.

But in truth, however eager a child may be to start school,

however much she or he has been prepared by the parent, teacher or older sibling, school and starting school is an unknown until it has been experienced. It is an idea, a fantasy and as such contains within it all the ghoulish and horrific emotional states found in fairy tales.

School in a child's mind is not necessarily a benign idea. Or, more accurately, it is not only a benign idea. It is also a worried-over idea. A child's imaginings, if addressed, listened to and not ridiculed, if empathised with rather than patronised, comforted rather than 'there-there-deared', have a chance to fade if the school environment indeed turns out to be benign, or – even better – good! But if a child's normal fears are pooh-poohed, the child is liable to develop anxieties which then need to be covered up. The effort the child engages in to protect itself from its anxieties saps its energy for social and educational tasks. The conditions for September melancholia as well as a fear of new things in general are laid down.

School fear is something we should expect our children to experience. It is one component of their experience, as valid and as important as their eagerness. If the parent and teacher can accept it, they can help the child accept it and integrate it as part of the mosaic of a big new experience. If we judge it, scorn or shame the child, we make it into a big deal and create a trauma where ordinary nervousness prevailed. As our little ones begin to absorb their new environments, let's be sure to make space for them to tell us the scary bits, the horrible bits, the sad bits about saying goodbye, about being there all day and about handling bumping up against twenty or thirty other little ones. Providing this emotional space avoids dread, fear and anxiety and allows them instead to approach beginnings with appropriate nervousness, pleasure and excitement.

Bad Results

Households with children may find July a rather testing time. The results of the SATs administered to 7-year-olds in state-sector schools have been collated and duly passed on to parents; older children and young adults have taken their GCSEs and A levels; the university exams are over and thousands of people await the results of their efforts.

For anyone who has lived through the system, these exams demarcate social relations. If we pass the correct number of exams and achieve sufficiently high grades, we have access to personal possibilities of an entirely different nature from those who do not.

Of course it it not passing exams *per se* that gives us access, confidence or feelings of entitlement to a piece of the wider world; it is the social milieu we come from, the way in which our society is structured, the educational institutions we pass through, the particular family relations at home, the encouragement or discouragement of others, and so on, that shape our place in the world and our relationship to those exams.

Ours is a deeply divided society, and our educational institutions play their part in these divisions. We are all too familiar with the social function of exams and the social results of passing and failing, but the psychological price we pay for an educational system still geared to inequality often passes unnoticed.

In my day, failure of the 11-plus relegated one not simply to diminished opportunities but in many instances to feelings of low self-esteem, of second-classness, of deficiency, of being somehow less worthy or valuable than others.

Breaking out of that legacy as an adult – daring to take a degree or do work that is highly regarded by society – can in turn be painful and difficult. Externally and internally branded, it can be hard to trust that what one has to offer is valuable, or what one feels interested in pursuing is within psychological reach.

These kinds of feelings are still rife. Despite the most thoughtful and creative efforts of teachers and educationalists, passing, or how we pass, what schools and colleges we attend, mark us externally and create or mirror internal states about our own worth. Exams and tests for many are far from being a chance to demonstrate what one knows. They are complex expressions of social and psychological pressures.

In Germany, a national telephone hotline has been set up for students suffering from stress in an attempt to counteract the rising trend of suicide attempts among young people around exam time. I know a PhD candidate who failed to open his mouth during his viva; of A-level students who turn up on the wrong days; of people who haven't slept easily for weeks in anticipation of the dreaded exams.

For some, taking exams is neither a challenge nor an ordeal. They encounter exams with little difficulty, enjoy the boundary of producing in such circumstances and perform reasonably. But for many, taking and passing exams is more than a physical and mental ordeal. It is as though their very essence is on the line.

Exams take on psychological meanings and purposes that have little to do with learning or creating. Of course there are many different ways in which exam tension can play out, but two fairly common examples are worth discussing.

Jonathan was, by all accounts, a successful student. He passed his O and A levels well and started on a maths degree. The competition at college was fierce; students jockeyed for position to work on the prof's interesting projects so that they could go on to post-graduate research and so on. Jonathan received his first and quickly went on to do his PhD.

The exams he encountered on the way were almost like a *raison d'être*. They organised his relationship to the work and each one became a huge challenge that excited and energised him. But once the exams were over and the results posted, Jonathan felt depressed and empty. The exams, rather than representing the consolidation of work well done, became devalued. If he could pass them, anyone could. They weren't worth that much.

So what is going on here? What turns these external markers into vacuous symbols for Jonathan? What are the psychological mechanisms at work that negate the academic success he has achieved?

For Jonathan, and many others, internal states of feeling inadequate or useless are temporarily eased by mobilising talents in an externally provided challenge. It is the challenge that gives Jonathan a sense of validity and aliveness, a sense of being able to contest the inner state of worthlessness. The achievement ends the challenge and depression follows until another external mountain can be found to climb. The need to master becomes the motivation for activities. Often, the achievement cannot be enjoyed in its own terms, for that was never its function. It was the risk that provided the buzz and as it is the risk that Jonathan thrives off, he needs to take ever increasing ones in order to feel alert and alive.

Sam's insecurity, on the other hand, expresses itself in exam phobia. Although now 50 and not needing to take exams any more, he frequently dreams of arriving in a strange city where he is expected to take an exam for which he is under-prepared. He can't find the exam hall, his pens and pencils don't work and he arrives late and sweaty with scant time available to take the test.

His schooldays were spent in a highly competitive atmosphere. While getting high marks was considered important, students lied to one another about how much studying they were really doing, disdaining the work on the one hand and swotting up on the other.

Sam's high marks allowed him to pass out of his social background and into an occupation quite outside familial expectations. For Sam, exams did symbolise worth and value. If he could get decent marks then his inner feelings of fraudulence, of not being in the right place, of not quite deserving what he was in fact having access to, could somehow be managed. The exam results could be used as an external point of validation, soothing feelings of dislocation and low self-esteem.

For parents, children's exam time is also trying. It is hard for parents not to project their own feelings on to their offsprings' attainments. Many a parent feels that her or his 7-year-old child's test results – however much they may have opposed the introduction of the tests for political or educational reasons – reflect their failure or achievement as parents.

GCSEs can embody the same parental projection. One chivvies the child to study, to put her or his all into the exam, to perform as one has performed or would have wished to perform. Their child's result becomes their result, their stamp of approval or disapproval. Meanwhile, children can feel that they are doing it for someone else, that they need to do well for Mum or Dad.

Feelings of self-worth, of being a valued member of society, of being able to act creatively thus become psychologically enmeshed in the testing situation. The destructive sense of being judged and found wanting or of using exams and tests as a mechanism to garner self-esteem, which is only replenished by turning all sorts of other activities into tests, raises important questions about the underlying feelings of distress so many people experience.

But it also raises important questions about an educational system that is once again gearing itself to testing. So I am suggesting two things. Exams both create distress and express latent distress. By being aware of the latent distress we can probably deal with exams in a less fraught way, but we still have larger cultural questions to address about the enormous social and psychological hurt exams can cause.

Fear of Intimacy

We celebrate the ease of love, but
for many of us attachment,
commitment and intimacy are
problematic.

Sex in the Long-term Relationship

While many couples continue to be actively sexual, many committed, nominally sexual relationships become distinguished by their lack of sexual acitivity. The couple still consider themselves a sexual couple and they rarely engage in a sexual liaison outside the relationship, but sex somehow gets less and less frequent, more predictable when it happens and loses its power to express the bond it once did.

While there are numerous jokes about why this happens, and lots of commonplace explanations ranging from fatigue to boredom to sexual disappointment, to anger in the relationship, to children, to in-laws, to work, to bad manners in bed, I want to explore the slowdown in sexual activity between a couple in a different way. What has been little explored is the way such a slowdown may at its heart express the difficulty with becoming more involved rather than presage the demise of intimacy.

James and Eleanor found that after ten years of being together their sexual activity had decreased and that when they did sleep together rows inevitably followed. They were still attracted to one another, enjoyed each other, shared common interests, were supportive of one another, talked intimately and in their mind's eye were still passionate about one another. But in practice, one would go off to bed earlier than the other, or one would have an important piece of work to do when the space might have been clear for a sexual encounter.

They were both aware of this phenomenon and, when apart, Eleanor found herself feeling really turned on when contemplating sex and resolved that tonight she wouldn't avoid it. James was perplexed. He enjoyed sex with Eleanor, yet he rarely picked up from her that she was interested and he was reluctant to push himself on her.

Sometimes they would joke about their lack of sexual activity; sometimes they would reassure one another that the reason they were having so little sex was that they had other ways to express and show their caring for one another; sometimes they put it down to the wish to savour sex and make it something out of the ordinary, something they would partake of on holiday but not on a routine basis; sometimes they thought that their internal image of themselves as parents precluded experiencing themselves as actively sexual people. But finally none of these explanations or adaptations satisfied them. They became compellingly aware of the fact that when they did engage in a good sexual encounter, distance – usually provoked by fighting – often ensued. This outcome then made them somewhat wary. They didn't understand the connection but they recognised that sex was followed by something disagreeable.

So what was going on? Why should good sex make them distant? What was it in their encounter that ruffled them? They knew it wasn't about disappointment in the actual sex: as they had come to know each other better over the years, aspects of their sex life had become less urgent, but other equally satisfying aspects had come to the fore and they knew a variety of ways to exchange pleasure.

What seemed to be going on was that the sexual encounter actually brought them to another level of intimacy. If they allowed themselves to recognise that they were making love to and with one another rather than successfully having orgasms they were moved to a deeper level of attachment. This recognition breached a barrier – a level of closeness at which they had stabilised – and instead of the sex complementing that level of closeness it pushed them towards a more intense and profound level of intimacy which unsettled the status quo.

When they had first been getting to know each other, sex had been a mechanism for closeness. Through it they shared the most intimate parts of themselves. At the beginning of their relationship they were prepared for the emotional upheaval that getting involved implied. They thrived on it, gave it lots of attention and experienced themselves opening up in new ways, discovering unknown aspects of self, and enjoying loving and being loved. As they found themselves committed to one another, new levels of intimacy were reached. But in time the attention to the couple that so marks beginnings in relationships gives way as the couple becomes less a private relationship and more a public fact.

Although James and Eleanor managed to protect and savour their intimacies for a considerable period, after a while they seemed to lose the ability to incorporate deeper intimacy and they held themselves, each one in their own skin and in their own space, at a particular level of closeness. When they broke through that level they became terribly frightened and immediately had to retreat to the position they were in before they had become too vulnerable. Being even closer made them psychologically uncomfortable.

James and Eleanor's experience is mirrored in many couples, whether heterosexual or homosexual. It seems that closeness needs to be balanced by a sense of separateness. But sex – the physical expression of the coming together of two separate people – can sometimes be *the* mechanism for psychically negotiating a comfortable level of closeness and separateness. Having more or less of it can act as a barometer of closeness.

James and Eleanor and many other couples feel that to open themselves up to the ecstatic or extraordinary aspects of sex disturbs the equilibrium of everyday life and is destabilising.

Sex pushes their relationship closer or, if that can't happen, then sex becomes deadened or interest pales.

Lack of sex then expresses not so much boredom but a fear of extending intimacy; a fear of personal boundaries being pierced; of extending closeness to an uncomfortable point. James and Eleanor needed to create an optimum level of closeness and distance. Passionate sex disrupted the manageable space between them and they unconsciously co-operated in fighting as a way to reposition themselves into a more manageable space. Like many couples they found it hard to integrate deeper levels of attachment. They didn't know how to balance increased closeness with maintaining a sense of personal boundaries and separateness.

Their challenge then was to allow passionate sex back into their lives without fearing that they would lose their individual selves or the capacity to be separate. By maintaining a physical separateness through forgoing sex they had bypassed the problem and unwittingly deprived themselves of sensual exchange. As they began to make love again more frequently they found other ways apart from fighting – usually talking – to regulate and digest the next level of intimacy it opened up. It wasn't that they couldn't achieve deeper intimacy. It was rather that they needed another means to accompany their sexual encounter in order to assimilate the deepening of their connection.

Valentines

For five hundred years, Valentine's Day has meant the secret dispatch of love greetings to a wished-for paramour, or the sending of hearts, flowers and sentiments of love to one's sweetheart. It is the day in the year dedicated to romantic love.

Like Mother's Day, Valentine's Day has been under attack for a couple of decades. Its ideological meanings have been picked over and deconstructed leaving romance somewhat dubious. But despite the onslaught, romance remains a compelling force and idea in many people's lives.

Much of women's fiction, women's magazines and the movie industry cater to (and to some extent create) the market for romance stories. Longing, heartache and union form the basis of the emotional plot. Avidly read and watched, romance stories in different guises tell us of separate lovelorn hearts finding one another. While the narrative focuses on the odds to be overcome so that lovers can come together, they stop at the point when togetherness has been reached. The reader or viewer is left to imagine the hearts-and-flowers future.

Romance is sold as the tantalising apex of experience, particularly for women. We rush to identify with the deep infatuation of two people exchanging interest, caring, love and attention. It warms us inside. We are left with the notion that life for both parties is at a new starting point. Each person's private self has been found, touched and revealed to the other. While undoubtedly gender divides some of our responses to romance (the search for adventure, the conquering of new vistas and the overcoming of adversity representing for many men an equivalent escape from the mundaneness of daily life) the romantic ideal shapes the sense of love, of relationship for us all.

Romance in itself is neither good nor bad. We invest in it and project on to it a variety of emotional needs. For lots of us, romance or the romantic phase of a relationship precedes the more humdrum work-a-day intimacies that are achieved in committed relationships. The memories of that early delicious contact; the capacity to open up and not simply reveal but discover new or dormant aspects of oneself; the delight in getting to know another's private self; the pleasure of erotic interchange; the capacity to experience love and to give it; all these underpin many people's attachments. Romance provides us with an emotional memory of what was possible and that remembrance can help us weather the misunderstandings and hard times in a relationship. We recall the energy once felt and hope to renew ourselves and our love through it.

But romance often doesn't turn into love. The enthralling interchange, with all its transcendent qualities, can vaporise as fast as it appeared. In place of love, there is a search for the feeling of being 'taken outside of oneself'. Romance becomes *the* experience. Walking on air, looking deep into another's eyes and living magical moments is what we crave. The companionate nature of many love relationships pales after the intensity of romantic experience.

But some people are trapped in the need to experience again and again the high of romance. It becomes a drug. Romance is the fix for the starved heart. But the very reasons why the intensity of romantic engagement is so craved make it unlikely that the needs behind the craving can be satisfied.

We can often observe that those who need repetitive romances choose for their partner one who is bound to disappoint them. Either they are drawn to mirror images of themselves or to someone whose bounded sense of self prevents them from dissolving into the other in the way the romance craver requires. What do I mean by this?

The need and the capacity to drown in another's eyes and soul for an extended period of time depends upon a self that is malleable and porous, a self which at the same moment as it reaches out to another to make an attachment, is searching for a connection that can enable it to develop further. The resources required to provide sustaining growth for one's own self are similar to the resources required to provide sustaining growth for another. If we can't provide it for ourselves, we will eventually find ourselves depleted in providing it for others.

In mirror-image romance, two people meet and for the period of intensity find parts of themselves that can love and be loved. But in time, unless this energy can be transformed into the stuff of everyday relating, both parties will be disappointed, feel empty and drained and disengage as they look for new sources of renewal.

If on the other hand the one who craves romance finds her or himself drawn to someone whose boundaries far from dissolving remain relatively impermeable, she or he may feel deeply frustrated as they try to get through the barriers. The barriers create the security that allowed the couple to become infatuated in the first place. The boundedness (or independence) of the other is reassuring. It feels solid. The solidity is something one wishes to lean on, to feed from, to grow from. But the solidity may not be yielding enough to provide the emotional nourishment, and even if it does, the person who craves may not believe that someone so solid can really love and appreciate them.

A process of unconscious underminding occurs. The apparently strong one is unconsciously dismantled inside the needy one's head, or their caring is considered inadequate. The barriers that were protective now feel excluding, and the romance withers.

Repeated encounters with both these kinds of partner can reinforce a sense of insatiability. One's need for love is endlessly stimulated, but because it is tied to romance it is also thwarted. Romance becomes a substitute, the bubble in which some love can be genuinely experienced but not sustained.

Romances can be wonderful preludes to relationships. But continually sought-after romances which fail can be thought of rather as attempts at love – encapsulating experiences of intimacy which let us know we need to understand better the impediments to attachment. On Valentine's Day we celebrate the ease of love, but for many of us attachment, commitment and intimacy are problematic. Demystifying some of the processes that occur in romance and understanding why desire evaporates rather than being transformed and consolidated into nourishing connection may help us struggle with the difficult psychological issues at hand.

Seriously Sexy

Sex in a new relationship along with its pleasures poses particular problems. When people first get together, sex becomes a major way in which they communicate, mark out their relationship as special and create a private world of joy. As we are coming to be more aware of the importance of safe sex, I want to extend that discussion to include the problems of creating emotionally safe sex as well as physically safe sex.

One of the important by-products of the fear engendered by sexually transmitted diseases is that we are learning to be more open as a culture about the practice and the mechanics of sex. Some explicit videos recently produced by the Terence Higgins Trust, *Seriously Sexy* (safer sex for young people), *Well Sexy Women* (a lesbian guide to sexual health), and *Getting It Right* (safer sex for young gay men), provide a way for new couples to talk about how to practise safe sex in seriously sexy ways.

These videos are helping breach the wall of secrecy that has surrounded sexual practices. The actual things people do with one another sexually are beginning to be talked about, described and shown, making it possible to think into a larger repertoire of sexual exchange while simultaneously reducing the shame that people often experience about their particular desires. As long as sexual practice is hidden in the closet, personal desire that doesn't fit the imagery of sexuality that has permeated our awareness can feel almost perverse. As sexually transmitted diseases seriously threaten our health, forcing us to explore and speak of our actual practices, we discover that there are an enormous variety of sexual practices. This discovery diminishes the burden of feeling perverse or unusual and allows us access to a more generous attitude towards our own sexuality.

The need for physically safe sex implicitly raises important gender and emotional issues. The still existing constraint on the expression of women's needs in general hampers their capacity to easily articulate what they like sexually, whether they are having sex with women or with men. The beginning of a relationship holds the promise that one will discover oneself anew within it and the hope that one's sexuality will not only be recognised but also extended.

But the beginning of a relationship is also a time of great delicacy and women schooled not to dare to show private aspects of self may feel extremely hesitant about disclosing disappointment. They may feel especially sensitive to the feelings of the other and hold back out of a fear that the expression of their desire will somehow represent an attack or a searing criticism of the other. Similarly, because of the conflictual messages about female bodies needing to conform to a particular aesthetic, girls continue to absorb the notion that their bodies and their passions are somehow not quite right. Women may be preoccupied about whether they can show what they want sexually and worry about whether what they look like while making love reflects received images of sexuality. These are specifically gendered issues alive for women that can make sex a quagmire. They require airing so that women are able to claim a pleasurable, shame-free sexual life.

For men, meanwhile, concern about safe sex has been a force helping to broaden male concepts of sexuality ranging from issues of performance to the necessity of penetrative sex. The pressure on men to 'perform', and the compulsion for many men to perform no matter what the circumstances, has limited men's sexual repertoire. Performance pressure, creating the idea that men are always ready for sex, has limited men's emotional repertoire. Frequently, sex for men comes to be used as a substitute for a whole range of feelings. Whether in heterosexual or homosexual liaisons, there is now far more opportunity for men to discuss both the physical and the emotional aspects of a sexual relationship. Sex can be moved ever so slightly off centre stage so that other forms of expression can be seen and developed.

The Freudian heritage that gave sexuality pride of place in human motivation has for the last hundred years competed with theological views which wish to contain sexuality in loving relationships. The important challenge to bourgeois morals that started as a broad movement in the 1960s, encompassing and often led by feminist or homosexual critiques, continues to force us to think about sexuality. The debates range from what sex and sexuality are, to whether sexuality is indeed polymorphously perverse or whether it is a channel of expression within relationships.

Many of us take sexuality as a given – whatever its form – without being much able to understand what it is. Is it a hunger like food, is it a biological imperative that will seek satisfaction by some means, is it a desire that arises within a particular relational context? In considering the conditions that make for emotionally safe sex, it seems that when people become sexually engaged, the feelings of vulnerability touched can be so profound that one needs a certain kind of emotional ambience, a sense of the possibility of an ongoing relationship, for the vulnerability that is felt to be contained and treasured.

Emotionally safe sex speaks to those aspects of sexuality that touch on the need for the relational aspects of erotic exchange rather than the purely corporeal. Opening up to another with one's body may bring up unexpected feelings that are extremely powerful. The erotic moves us in ways we can't foresee and the ability to feel safe, rather than threatened and ashamed, may depend on the openness of one's partner. Although emotionally safe sex can occur in relationships that are at different levels – from potentially committed to casual encounters – a feature of all of them is a symmetry between the needs of the parties. If for many people emotionally safe sex requires the context of a loving relationship then this has to be respected. The struggle to articulate that need is as crucial as the struggle to articulate the necessity of using condoms and other barriers.

There is still pressure on young women to show their feelings for their men by being prepared to have unprotected sex. Where thirty years ago, the pressure to abandon physical barriers endangered women in one way, it now endangers both parties. But there is still an uncomfortable power dynamic when a woman accedes to potentially unsafe sex. Her willingness to do this is often exploited as she interprets the man's request to give up protection as a positive indication of his commitment. But physically unsafe sex then becomes a dangerous vehicle. It may give a temporary but illusory feeling of emotional safety.

AIDS and our greater access to understanding sexual practice whether heterosexual or homosexual is giving us ways to understand more about sex, sexuality and sexual practices. Let's make sure that the issues of emotionally safe sex form part of the conversation too.

Dancing in the Dark

Intimacy is indeed a most devilish state. At the beginning of a love affair we experience bliss. We feel able to reveal ourselves, to share, to feel the joy of mutual pleasure. Our erotic desires are stimulated. We fantasise that our longings for our most private selves to be seen and understood will be recognised.

The experience of having another riveted on us – apparently selflessly – can feed and warm the hungry self. But is that mutually exchanged attention real recognition? Or does the desire to give and receive attention lead us into a state in which reality and fantasy are indiscernible? Does the recognition we crave prevent us from seeing the many unconscious projections we elicit and engage in? Does it mean that we might see what isn't there? And we might not see what is there? When we are infatuated we imagine unconditional love and acceptance. But there is a large gap between that experience and the feelings that can occur once we are entrenched in a relationship. Although we might anticipate that security comes with familiarity, often in a well established relationship we can imagine rejection and restriction where it may not exist. The intimacy we yearn for turns out to be problematic.

167

Our experience of intimacy, of closeness, of love, is power-fully shaped by our gender and the fact that we are, for the most part, mother-reared. We first experience love in a one-to-one relationship with our carer and the emotional ambience of that very first relationship stays with us almost as a blueprint for intimacy.

If we have come from secure homes in which we have felt loved and appreciated, we grow up with a belief that who we are and what we bring to relationships is valuable. We are generally secure in feeling that what we find in relationships will be satisfactory. We are able to weather conflicts and differing desires without feeling that the relationship or our-selves is at risk. We are confident about our capacity to love and to be loved and we unconsciously seek to mirror the positive emotional states that we have lived in before. We know them and we derive a certain safety from them.

But this is the ideal. The impossible pressure on mothers who by and large have sole unsupported responsibility for parenting means that it is hard for many of us to grow up feeling quite so secure.

Often the needs we have as a child can't be fulfilled. And when this happens and we don't understand *why* they aren't being met, we absorb the idea that our desires, hungers, wants and aspirations are wrong. We are susceptible to feeling angry, hungry, undeserving, insatiable, empty and despairing. We have little confidence that what we bring to relationships, who we are, is either worthy or capable of being understood.

We will be drawn towards relationships that seem to be able to make up for the void, the nothingness, the bad feelings inside. We will seek relationships which can mitigate our insecurities, fill the hole inside, allow us to be filled up with love.

And then, if we are unused to consistent love, to the experience of closeness, the very thing we crave also terrifies us. Love feels unfamiliar. It is hard to assimilate, to believe in. When we encounter it, we may unconsciously push it away, reject it. We bring our insecurities, our historic feelings of insatiability, anger and hurt, our belief that we are undeserving, to the present relationship and imagine that we are about to be abandoned, if not now then later.

The difficulty we have with intimacy is in part due to the fact that women are the sole, isolated, caretakers of our children, a fact that produces a very different dynamic for boys and girls. In our society, girls are raised to be the givers and nurturers of *others*. Girls learn to create relationships in which others can depend on them. They are not brought up to expect this kind of nurture themselves; they are encouraged to deny their own needs and convert them into meeting the needs of others.

This denial doesn't stop a girl's desire for closeness and nurture. Although her first relationship with her mother leaves her upset, and feeling rage and disappointment, she attempts in adult life to solve this dilemma by latching on to another, hoping to become so close that the two separate identities will merge into one. But once 'close' she unconsciously imagines and projects rejection and finds it hard to believe that she is loved.

Boys are raised to expect emotional nurturance and attention without being aware that it is being given. Rarely are they encouraged to focus on others in this way themselves. Indeed, in their attempt to create a masculine identity they may flee from identification with the feminine. Rather than merging with others they create boundaries between themselves and others, through the processes of disidentification and differentiation. Closeness with a woman then can be extremely threatening. For it stirs up his own very early experience with his mother. In so far as that was problematic, then the development of a masculine sense of self, of difference, of opposition, was a refuge from those difficulties. The legacy of being mother-reared is that he unconsciously both idealises and fears his mother. These twin feelings are in turn unconsciously projected on to women he becomes close to.

In other words, I think it would be fair, if somewhat of a

generalisation, to say that a man bolsters his identity by distancing and appearing not to need, while a woman seeks to solve the problems of her identity by Velcro-ing herself to another. As a man and a woman attempt to become intimate, the legacy of their earliest intimacies are stimulated. Between women lovers these dynamics play out rather differently, but a fear of intimacy can be just as present. While both women are able to provide for the dependency needs of one another and both may crave it, both may also be unused to receiving this kind of continuing care. It can feel too cloying. Without the boundary that gender creates, the distance between lovers that is needed to maintain intimacy has to find a way of being psychologically structured. If women cannot participate equally in creating that distance between them while simultaneously holding on to desired closeness, the space is sought either through one woman becoming more clingy while the other is freer to feel independent, or by a third person – a new lover or very close friend – becoming important to one of the women. All these factors can make for a fairly lethal fit within intimate relationships, a pronounced cha–cha–cha, each person moving forwards and backwards without quite meeting the other, leaving tremendous misunderstanding, disappointment, isolation, hurt and loneliness.

Dissecting these tragic heterosexual mismatchings of masculinity and femininity can produce quite a gloomy picture. But if we are to alleviate the distress that can pervade relationships after the first bloom of love has faded, we need to look at these processes, and to take account of the way in which gender is currently constructed.

Many couples could get out of the 'she's too dependent and he's so withdrawn', or 'now he's demanding and she's distant' dance if they recognised the way in which dependency needs are unconsciously batted back and forth between partners rather than shared.

Needs, vulnerability, dependency have become dirty words in our culture. We have developed elaborate psychological defences against experiencing them directly. These defences then keep us estranged from ourselves and our loved ones; they make us fearful of such feelings and contemptuous of their expression. We often find ourselves rejecting such feelings in ourselves and resisting their display in others. As a result potential intimacy can ring alarm bells and we resurrect our defences.

We need to acknowledge, then face individually and as couples, our very real fears of intimacy and of dependence. We need to accustom ourselves to the idea that needs, dependencies, vulnerabilities are simply that – not good, not bad. They are just a fact of relationships. If dependency needs can be shared then instead of the cha-cha-cha, with one person feeling insecure and the other feeling threatened and having to keep at a distance, the chasm between two people can begin to be bridged and an intimacy in which common needs can be recognised is possible.

The Tyranny of Togetherness

The theme of insecurity runs through many of these articles because it is so basic to the problems that bring people to psychotherapy. A difficulty in believing that one is worthy and lovable can lead to a tortuous set of psychological 'manoeuvres' that play havoc with relationships. These unconscious manoeuvres seem destined to destabilise a loving relationship.

Gina and Chris had been together for a year. They were both students from troubled families who in finding one another felt understood, loved and cared for. They enjoyed each other greatly, were passionately involved but their relationship would go through testing times every eight weeks or so when an explosion would erupt between them leading both of them to feel like separating. In between these bouts, Gina moved in and out of feeling more or less secure. Chris felt wonderful as long as they weren't fighting.

A typical row would start over something apparently trivial. One Friday night, Chris and Gina were spending the evening together. At 9.30 p.m. Chris's good friend Mike rang up to ask Chris out for a drink in half an hour. Chris asked Gina whether she would mind. Gina did mind, but she didn't know why and

173

she didn't think it was right to mind. Although she and Chris had planned to spend the evening together Mike had just returned from six months away so she didn't want to be unreasonable and possessive. Because she felt complicated about her feelings she told Chris it was fine, but she found herself withdrawn and sulky. Chris kept badgering her about whether it was really all right until, feeling besieged, she blurted out that it wasn't.

Chris felt uneasy about going out, told Mike that he would see him in the morning and went back to his evening with Gina. She remained distanced and the next morning when they parted they had a row. Chris said he would ring about getting together in the afternoon, she said not to bother, and he didn't.

After he left the flat Gina felt remorse. She had been angry with him but felt her response was unjustified. She blamed herself for being such a bitch, so unreasonable, for feeling so threatened, and instead felt guilty and sorry that she had provoked a bad scene. She hoped Chris would ring so that she could make amends. She wanted to suggest that she would make a late lunch for herself, Chris and Mike.

In the event, Chris failed to ring and by the time he turned up at 5.00 p.m. Gina was angry again. She'd been through a wringer of emotions, from anger to guilt to sorrow and remorse, and now she felt betrayed all over again. She had wanted to give, to show her love, to show her acceptance of the rightness of Chris seeing his friend, but those feelings had evaporated in the face of his late return.

As Gina told it, the story was all about her unreasonableness: she was so insecure, so distrustful that she would destroy the relationship. With this as the explanation there wasn't much more for Gina to do than curb her temper and watch out for her withdrawn state. But this stance couldn't work: simply policing her emotions wasn't going to stop the eruptions. And of course this explanation was too limited. It didn't look at Gina and Chris as a couple. It saw only her role in the rows rather than seeing that they were the outcome of unconscious moves between the two of them.

Gina's legacy from childhood was one of feeling insecure and unlovable. Only if she were closely attached to Chris could she feel some safety and security. Chris's childhood legacy had been feelings of guilt when he wanted to do things separately from Gina so that he felt he was abandoning her, hurting her, every time he went out without her. Coupled to this was an enormous resentment that *she* was making him feel this way.

Chris tried to deal with his dilemma by getting Gina's permission – almost her blessing – to go out separately and then when he was away 'forgetting' about her and the arrangements they had made. Inevitably on meeting again there would be a row and he would feel punished for having left her.

What tipped us off to the shared responsibility of this pattern of interaction was Chris's observation that much as he loathed the punishing rows, he anticipated them and felt strangely relieved when they occurred. It was as though he was enacting a pattern in which he must pay a price for having a life that was separate from Gina's. In his insecurity, he couldn't accept that Gina would support his friendships and separate activities and so he would unconsciously set her up to punish him, to restrict him, to make his unease about *his* separateness her fault. At the same time, her outbursts or withdrawal showed how much she cared, and so he could feel both wanted and rejecting at the same time. She was expressing her need for him so he didn't have to face the difficulty he experienced in being loved when he wanted to be apart.

Gina didn't want to be put in the position of being the one who was preventing him from doing what he wanted. His insistent questions about whether it was all right or not for him to go out set up difficult feelings in her. It played on her conflict about how to handle closeness and separateness. It clashed with her idea about trust and mutual support. She needed her psychological energy to cut into feelings of insecurity that were activated when separation loomed. That insecurity, when paramount, propelled her to construct scenarios of abandonment; to see Chris as betraying her; to envisage an inevitable end to the relationship. It prevented her from accepting the love and commitment Chris offered. Gina knew that she needed to get far enough past her insecurity to allow the relationship that *actually* existed between them to nourish and sustain her. She felt she could take responsibility for working on her own insecurity if she didn't also have to respond to Chris's agenda – his feeling that he was betraying her when he left to do something separately.

She wanted him instead to consult her about arrangements in advance so that it was a mutual decision that didn't require permission. His persistent checking made her doubt herself: it suggested to her that perhaps something wasn't all right and that she should worry. Even more importantly, it placed her in the position of his keeper – a position that demeaned her. She asked him to consult her next time, not to exclude her and then seek her sanction, but to discuss it before and then accept her support for his activities.

Chris, for his part, tried to change his tendency to make a quasi-covert arrangement that he then had to confess and get permission for. He was going to risk saying directly what he wanted and take responsibility for it.

Although neither Gina's nor Chris's insecurities dissolved instantly, their ability to disentangle their historic insecurity from what they actually needed from each other in the present cleared a space for them to enjoy each other and feel unthreatened by each other's separate activities. They found a way to expose their vulnerabilities more honestly. Gina learnt to say when she felt insecure, and Chris could reassure her. He talked with her about his feelings of guilt that he was abandoning her when he wanted to be separate and he could see that while these feelings were evoked for him in the relationship, Gina was not causing them, so she was not responsible for them.

Tangles like these in relationships are rarely instigated or perpetuated by one person. We have a funny knack in intimate relationships of binding with partners who almost exquisitely stimulate our insecurities. Chris found a way to make his lover possessive. Gina found Chris's exclusion and then beseeching excruciating. Whatever the dynamic between a couple, bringing it to awareness and thinking about how each party reacts to the problem can begin the unravelling of each person's part in the psychological fit. That process can dissolve the interlock and allow the insecurity to be processed rather than continually re-enacted.

Damaging Relationships

All of us have had women friends, family members, colleagues or clients who seem unable to extricate themselves from relationships that are desperately bad for them, that hurt them and seem to bring them little pleasure.

It is confusing when we can see little objective reason standing in the way of their getting out and into a better situation. Positioned outside, we are perplexed and find it hard to imagine what is so compelling for the woman involved.

So how can we better understand what's going on? How can we understand what keeps women in bad relationships?

In working with women who stay in damaging relationships the psychotherapist often discovers that her patient has a history of abusive relationships both inside and outside her family of origin. For women with this history, relationship is equated with abuse. The most intimate, the most significant, the most compelling of relationships that the woman has experienced have been characterised by abuse.

Love – perhaps attention is a better word – has come in the form of abuse, invasion and exploitation. The most profound way the woman, as a girl, has been seen and noticed has been as an object for someone else, as a thing to be used by them, as a victim. Since this may be the only form of contact she has, it can be both dreaded and desired. The girl may fear the abuse and yet at another level feel needed. At the same time, the badness she feels inside as someone who has been brutally disregarded and trampled on makes her feel that *she* is at fault for participating in the activity.

Jenny, now 50, was sexually abused by her grandfather, who lived next door, from the ages of 8 to 12. She is the mother of two children, a son of 18 and a daughter of 22. Brought up in the 1950s she had what appeared to be a conventional middle-class early adult life. After teacher-training college, she taught for a while, married, and when her children came along she ceased work outside the home until they were in secondary school. Her husband's career took him all over Europe so she was responsible for managing the domestic, educational and social arrangements in all the cities they lived in.

Although her husband has the capacity to be kind and charming, more often he acts a brute and is difficult to live with. He ridicules her in public, fails to consult her on major decisions that affect her life and has the capacity to make her feel quite bad about herself. If the food he requires is not on the table, he'll overturn the table. When the children had difficulties with their homework, he blamed her for being lackadaisical. If he doesn't like what she's wearing he calls her a whore, an ugly bitch. If she laughs when he wanted a different kind of response, he'll verbally threaten her.

He's a volatile man, hugging the children one moment and berating them for insolence the next. When he is at home there is an air of fear and Jenny spends a good deal of her energy trying to assess his mood so that she doesn't inadvertently trigger his violence.

Although Jenny is scared of her husband and often angry with him she feels trapped – not in an economic or social sense but because she has internalised notions about herself that make it almost impossible for her to conceive of a better life. She cannot imagine living a life in which she has personal control. Jenny feels like an empty shell – a fraud. She is so used to suiting herself to the prevailing social climate, to finding a part of herself that can survive any encounter or social grouping, that she despairs of knowing who she is unless she is reacting to others.

The only known and continuous idea of self that she holds is a strong sense of her shortcomings. She feels that it is *her* fault her husband is irascible. She should be able to control these moods. It is her responsibility to create a harmonious family and if there are eruptions, it is her fault: she didn't handle him properly, she didn't take account of the pressure he is under at work, she didn't sufficiently see things from his point of view.

Following a fight, Jenny continually replays in her mind agonising, punishing, ritualised scripts which berate her for *her* inadequacy and her inability to do the right thing. She has many 'if only' scenarios: if only I hadn't offended him, if only I were more intellectual, or if only I had warned the children that Daddy was on the warpath and so on. As we talk we discover that the function of these deeply hurtful self-inflicted attacks is to ameliorate the most agonising feelings of powerlessness and helplessness.

Jenny, like many women who have been abused, finds these feelings excruciating. The actual powerlessness such women feel and walk around with is so hurtful that they substitute another feeling, a feeling that it is all their fault, which gives them some relief. For if it was their fault then there is something they could have done about it. The helplessness felt deep down is so appalling that it is converted into feeling that one must somehow have caused it. Whatever is wrong, whatever was wrong, is somehow something that one occasioned.

Behind the present savage self-flagellation is a thought which Jenny can't bear to encounter but which haunts her: that she is responsible for the abuse she experienced as a child. She caused it, she could have done something about it. She is guilty. But this idea is difficult too and becomes transposed into taking responsibility now, as an adult, for everything else in the world. She is responsible for her husband's emotional state and his attacks on her. The neglect and abuse she suffered as a child has made her feel compelled to take on the responsibility for others' lives and to protect them from hurt. When she fails at this, she suffers deeply.

The unconscious guilt which pushes her to take the blame for everything around her, competes with a contradictory but almost equally forceful idea: that it is all his fault/her mother's fault/her grandfather's fault. She is a victim but again this idea is indigestible because it makes her feel trapped, so she repositions her perceived complicity at the centre of the drama and creates a scenario where she could have done better. The cycle continues.

This not uncommon set of psychic gymnastics means that Jenny isn't able to enjoy much of her life. Although she has material comfort, children who are doing well, and a job that she is interested in, she finds it difficult to live in the present. She suffers painful oscillations between reiterating the past and projecting horror on the future. Nothing in her everyday life today gives her much satisfaction. She is one of the thousands and thousands of deeply unhappy women who seek help.

As she can slowly face the horror of her past and from the vantage point of her relative security live through again the feelings of rage, of fear, of terror that dominated her early years, she can release herself from the obsession and self-blame that colour her present life. While she may not be able to leave her husband, she will begin to contest his unreasonableness and stand up for herself in the relationship rather than take the blame and continually readjust.

Violent Connections

I have written about the damaging effects that childhood sexual abuse can have on adult life. Now I want to suggest how a cycle of violent and abusive relationships can start to be broken.

Sally is in an actively abusive relationship. Her husband drinks himself into violence, rapes her regularly, lies to her and steals her money. She contemplates leaving for the sake of the kids, but with few financial means and very low self-image, the effort seems monumental.

Sally lives a kind of split experience. On the one hand is her real experience of her husband, which is as a brute. She is angry, contemptuous, she knows he's a shit and so on. On the other hand, she lives in a daydream in which life turns out fine. Her man is a good guy who understands her and protects her. Somewhere inside herself, Sally invents a relationship of peace and contentment, a relationship which nourishes her and lets her give and receive love. Positioned here, soothing herself with the fantasy of a caring relationship, she is brought up short by the reality of who he actually is and how he relates to her. When he then fails to meet her unconscious expectations it is as though he has fallen off his white horse and become the contemptible, hateful bastard.

Because Sally is unaware of how in her own mind she has recreated him as someone really very different than who he is, she can't recognise her disappointment with the real him or the extent to which she has created him in fantasy. What she can do – and this is especially painful – is cover her disappointment with rage and then find a form of contact in the rage. It is not that she provokes violence; but when it occurs its familiarity provides a release of tension and a known, certain form of contact. In it she reiterates intense emotional states from her childhood.

When the bout of violence is over, Sally returns in her mind to that space she has created in which flowers and love predominate. She copes with her longing for a loving relationship by making up one for herself. The problem with this adaptation is that it doesn't allow her to live in the present in her existing relationship. She is always caught short by it and then moves into a different mode, a mode of hate, rage and contempt.

It is very easy to think that the rage Sally expresses is productive. And of course at one level it is. But at another level, her rage, rather than allowing her to detach from the situation, to separate herself from her man, acts as a kind of glue. It is her part of the adhesive in a relationship characterised by violence. The rage is the place where she makes a connection with her husband.

Sally, and other women I have worked with who have been abused or are now in abusive relationships, is enormously creative. These women construct narratives and lives for themselves that to some extent allow them to continue to live with the most unbearable situations and psychic pain. But these adaptations based on denial, reconstruction and fantasy are, of course, only creative up to a point. They are partial solutions which, while they keep the woman either prepared for the worst or make her think she is matching her feelings of powerlessness with feelings of power, hardly enable her to extract herself from the situation. And often even if she is able to extricate herself from such a relationship, she may find herself in another where the shadings and particulars may be different but which contains extremely similar psychological components.

We know that in order for systematic abuse to have occurred in childhood or adolescence, we can presume a situation in which the person abused was unable to let it be known. There was no adult who could either countenance what the child said and step in and do something about it, or the child felt too afraid to tell anyone. The absence of a reliable adult means that it is extremely unlikely that the abused person could ever find her way to a trusting relationship with another.

So what is needed for Sally and others in similar circumstances to free themselves from repeated patterns of abuse? What Sally needs is a place where the hurt, the feelings of disappointment, personal badness, deep shame and culpability can be explored, a place where she can allow them to be felt. But her problem is compounded by the fact that she is unused to having anyone listen to her and engage with her. Her own thoughts, words and desires have been denied an audience for so long that she has felt socially and psychologically invisible.

She is unused to believing that what she says and how she feels about it matters. She is unused to trusting another adult to be there for her, to hear her experience and to tolerate the feelings she has had. Now she and others with similar histories need someone to stand by them, to bear witness, to accept and receive the pain and the rage they have been trying to keep at bay.

What adds to the conundrum is that women who have been abused feel great shame. This shame, instead of being attached to the perpetrator, taints the abused. In turn the shame acts as a shield against exploring many of the other feelings associated with repeated abuse. If the abused can recognise that shame, accepting that the feeling of being responsible is part of what often goes along with being abused then it may be easier to bear it rather than feel bound in by it. Shame, guilt, anger, despair and fear are some of the almost inevitable feelings that flow from being in a repeatedly abusive situation. They are part of the operation of the psyche's immune system (just as aching is a symptom of influenza). They alert, protect and inform us about practices that are indeed unendurable. They aren't stigmas but the psyche's way of coping with unbearable pain and invasion.

The woman who has been sexually abused, the woman who has been psychically abused, the woman who lives in a damaging relationship is often deeply unaware of her own power. She conceives of it only destructively and never as anything of use to her. But this power could be used to enable her to understand herself better, to discover what motivates her, to see what she desires, to dare to know what she wants. It could help her live with the pain of what she doesn't have, rather than remaking her current situation in her head over and over again as though she could fix the past. She can't – but if she can face it, then she has a chance to have some power in the present.

The Long Distance Love

At the start of the academic year, many students find themselves living in different cities from their boyfriends, girlfriends or partners. Both new and well established relationships face the problems of continuing at a distance. The challenges are many, including developing ways of communicating at long distance, keeping oneself open to the new experiences at college, and solving the emotional problems of repeated separations. But before these challenges can be faced, one must also consider the wider emotional circumstances in which the commuting relationship is to be conducted.

Starting college can be an exciting and rich experience; a time of great promise. But while lots of recognition is given to the benefits and privilege of going to college, and to how one has deserved to go to college, very little attention is paid to more problematic aspects. Precisely because college holds the hope of growth it can also be a scary time: there may be nervousness and fear about leaving home and entering an unfamiliar environment without friends and family.

Interestingly, shortly before starting further education, many young people find themselves falling in love or having their first serious sexual relationship. It is as though the psychologically monumental step of leaving home is eased by intense involvement with someone outside the family. The love affair provides the bridge out of the family as the young man or woman recasts its primary attachment. A psychic break with the family of childhood is then begun, but if the couple now find themselves separated in different cities it can affect how they approach and experience college. The security the relationship offered can be undermined and they can be confused about how to conduct themselves. Even with plans to write, telephone and visit, the heartbreak is considerable. There may be feelings of insecurity and feelings of loss. And these are sometimes compounded by parental attitudes which tend to belittle the relationship, stressing instead the importance of studying.

The difficult feelings to do with leaving home and starting university are played out around the drama of the lovers' impending separation. This may take the weight of all the issues the individual is facing, concealing other concerns about studying or the shift from the protected environment of home, from a city, town or village one knows well, from known relationships and understood obligations and reponsibilities.

Chris and Gail met at evening school in their early twenties. Together for two years, they both applied to university in their home town but Gail got her third choice (London) which was too far for her to commute to daily and would mean the disruption of their life together in Leeds. She needed to find accommodation, a new part-time job and so on, but more significantly she needed to reorientate herself and decide whether she was primarily based in Leeds and was in London during the week or whether she was establishing a separate home and life outside of the couple.

The initial panic and dismay led Gail to consider postponing studying for a year. She feared that Chris would find someone else, that she would be exhausted from weekend commuting, that she'd be hesitant to involve herself fully with college because part of her would be both physically and mentally in Leeds.

188

When Gail had first heard the news about getting a place at London she had been enormously upset, and felt annoyed with Chris because he didn't seem to be expressing much distress about the separation. She took his comparative reticence and lack of response as a sign of his indifference. And without checking this out, her insecurity led her to believe that he cared less and was even quite relieved that she would be leaving. Feeling this way she then developed a revenge scenario in which she would establish an entirely self-contained and separate life, date other students and stay in London at weekends, absorbing herself in college life.

She created this fantasy as a salve to her hurt feelings. Instead of engaging with her fears about the possible loss of Chris she envisaged a life which in its exclusion of him bypassed the substantial difficulties that faced them both. Not only did they need to talk about how to reassure one another and how to manage the demands of a relationship in which they would constantly be saying goodbye or hello, Gail also needed to talk about her own fears about going to a new place as an attached person who would be entering student life both bolstered and encumbered by her relationship with Chris. She was not going to London free to enter all that the university and city had to offer, for she had self-imposed emotional and geographical (commuting) constraints. What became clearer in time too was that her anxieties about going to university as a mature student had been hidden under the cover of her relationship. If she and Chris were together then she felt able to manage this new endeavour: she would have him to share and process it with. If they were separated then she feared her ability to manage all she'd be experiencing on her own. She felt nervous without Chris's emotional support.

Chris's reticence had come from his own fear and insecurity. He felt very lucky to have hooked up with Gail. He often felt very guilty and bad for needing her so much and he couldn't imagine – despite her protestations – that she wouldn't find someone else in London. He was gripped by insecurity and by shame about his dependence on her, and because he couldn't bear to expose it to her (or even himself, really) he withdrew. He was hiding his feelings and trying to deny them so that he would better cope with the loss of Gail that he felt was impending.

Like many couples, they got through this initial impasse and articulated their continued commitment to one another. Then the difficulty shifted. In order for each of them to survive without the other during the week they discovered that they shut down almost as though they had severed their link. Phone calls were tense and when they met on Fridays they felt nervous, shy and scared. They had to find a way to melt their emotional armouring and be open to one another again. But this wasn't easy. Misunderstandings and disappointments occurred. Each had a tendency to accuse the other of failing to reach out, and the weekends were tense rather than restorative. Eventually they realised that they established a pattern of fighting when getting together before they could become close, and fighting again when they were about to part. Although this didn't entirely dissolve once they realised how hard they found the process of re-entry and re-engagement, they found the mental space to minimise what was so difficult. They took care to share their vulnerability on re-entry and to say how shy and expectant they felt. They made specific times to speak in the week so as to be sure of connecting even when apart.

These strategies acknowledged the difficulties implicit in staying emotionally open to one another while absorbing new and separate environments. It allowed them to trust what had built up between them rather than jettison it. After the initial problems posed by commuting, Gail and Chris found ways to support each other and juggle the physical and emotional demands of a separate and committed life.

The problems Chris and Gail face exemplify those that arise in all commuting relationships. When the relationship is an established one the resources can be found to deal with and resolve the tensions created by new situations and distance. In new relationships, frequently undertaken as a response to the fears of leaving home, it can often be best to recognise that the relationship cannot support the enforced separations and that each person has to face the loss and establish a new life for themselves.

The Well of Solitude

Breaking up a relationship can be one of the most difficult emotional experiences of adult life. Among the many feelings that must be negotiated are intense feelings of loss, guilt towards the other party, rage, disappointment, and personal failure.

At the beginning of a relationship, when we are infatuated or falling in love, great hope and wonderment infuses the marvel of life and love. Our capacity to give, to be interested in everything about another, is enhanced and we experience the pleasure of being loved, of having a very special kind of attention focused on us. We find precious moments in the mutual exposure of vulnerability, in the sharing of intimacies, in introducing one another to our personal view of the world, our likes and dislikes, our charms and our joys. And we start the process of creating a shared world with common understandings and one another as a reference point.

In time the relationship becomes normalised and the very things we so valued in that initial period are transformed into the smaller intimacies and the hassles of everyday life and everyday relating. If we are lucky the everydayness is nourishing and sustaining. But if it fails to be so we may lust after the intoxicating feelings alive in the beginning of the relationship, hoping they will be revived and rescue us from the problems of day-to-day life.

When relationships fail – through misunderstandings, through betrayal, through incompatibility – we face the loss of hope and promise that getting together implied. We may feel a pull to re-romanticise the relationship, recalling its beginning stages and forgetting the pain and agony that fostered the break-up. The tasks of separating, making a new life, restructuring an identity outside of a primary adult attachment, and repositioning oneself with family, friends and children are extremely difficult. While our culture valorises love, romance and getting together, it has only informal support for those who are engaged in the process of breaking up.

Although there is much tut-tutting today about the frequency of break-ups and the lack of commitment that divorce and separation imply, in my experience breaking up is always a last-ditch option rather than a lightly taken solution. In the intervals between the wish to break up, the decision to break up and the actual break-up, there is much toing and froing and many attempts either to repair the relationship or to bury what is not right and start over again.

Breaking up is first and foremost a loss. It is akin to bereavement but often more difficult to come to terms with. Accepting the painful finality of death is ultimately what helps people to grieve and so to heal; to start life again without the loved one's presence. In separation, by contrast, the wish to connect or reattach can be stimulated again and acted upon many times over many years before there is a resolution. If children are involved, there is not just the experience of seeing one another but the conflicting desire to act in the children's best interests and to get away from and even to punish or hurt the other.

If both people live in a small community or work in the same place the distance that can often be helpful in creating a new life and an identity as a now de-coupled self may well be missing so that the constant exposure to one another can exacerbate the problems of separation. This can be particularly acute in sections of the lesbian community where the very marginalisation of homosexuality means one's community is smaller to begin with. If one temporarily divorces oneself from the social venues and friendship networks as a way of allowing the process of separation one may find oneself not simply out of a couple but deeply isolated too. This is also true for heterosexual women in middle age who are divorced (and widowed). Such women may find that their social networks are couple orientated, and may find themselves excluded from their social scene.

For many the process of breaking up is so excruciating that it can barely be envisaged. The pain of loss can put one in touch with deep feelings of emptiness that were not only mitigaged but obscured by a close attachment. These return with a vengeance with the threat and eventuality of loss, and can be so painful that we may find ourselves trying to alleviate them. Instead of a clean break-up, a new lover enters the picture who serves the function of easing the pain of aloneness, delaying the process of coming to terms with loss and with the need to establish an identity separate from one's partner.

Other couples whose sexual relationship may have lapsed for years find their passion reignited. The threat of loss puts them in touch with their desire, a desire that can only be felt when confronted with the potential emptiness that accompanies a tenuousness in their relationship. The same fervour that drives a re-eroticising of the relationship can be found in the desperate need to reach the departing other by almost any means. The frustration at not being heard and understood and the need to expose the pain one feels may push either party towards violence. This violence is motivated by desperation. It is an attempt more to reach out and expose the hurt than to punish. In a curious way, the couple breaking up may be closer to one another than they have been for ages. In their separate spheres they experience a similar anguish but ironically they cannot be of much help to each other in this process since what each needs to do is to face the aloneness and separation.

This is true for both people, whoever initiated the separation. It is rare for couples to decide to separate amicably and agreeably even when the relationship works for neither party. More commonly one person sees her or himself as the abandoned or betrayed one while the other person suffers guilt. Mixed in with feelings of loss are powerful feelings of anger, victimisation, personal failure and hurt. The tumultuous inner turmoil propels many separations towards bitter rows, with each party trying to damage and hurt the other. The feelings that are too much to bear make each one lash out at the other in an effort to bring the inner turmoil under control. If blame can be apportioned, if hurt can be expelled in the form of rage, if insecurity can be ameliorated by finding a new lover, then the feelings of emptiness and loss and the fear of a new beginning can be temporarily stilled.

What helps in breaking up is a reminder that there isn't much to do except to grieve and hurt. Blame may alleviate some hurt, anger may account for felt injustice, a new lover may postpone the recognition of aloneness. But it takes a very long time to 'get over' a relationship. When we've opened ourselves up emotionally to another, detaching is far from trivial. We are almost bound to try to resurrect it, to fantasise its revival, to rewrite its history. But the more we can face the loss directly and accept that it is going to hurt like nothing else, the more strength we will have to encounter the allied feelings of alienation, confusion, emptiness and fear accompanying the loss.

Final Chapter

Whether we are the Duke and Duchess of York or just plain old you and me, breaking up is difficult and painful. Often we try to manage that pain by telling ourselves a story about the relationship that temporarily soothes us. We hate our partner and we are relieved to get out; we were brutalised by his or her cruelty, we were betrayed or exploited; we were the victim of his or her midlife crisis, and so on.

The stories we tell ourselves about our relationship and its demise are important in many ways because how we explain that particular relationship to ourselves, to our friends, families and children, and the way our ex-partner sees 'our' version deeply influences the way in which we approach new partners or the way we live our lives on our own.

In so far as we situate ourselves as the 'wronged' party or the 'betrayer', or if we write a story of blame and victimisation – a device we may employ to solve the difficult experiences of ambivalent longing and loss – we will take such a picture of ourselves into our next relationships. There we may find ourselves either reiterating the same position or in the designated shoes of our ex-partner. Guilt and casualty, two of the emotional positions most often grafted on to the story of the ending of a relationship, are not however very useful concepts when trying to create a new life. Where guilt and victimisation bind up complex sets of feelings by either over-inflation or negation of responsibility, they often conceal much more complicated interpersonal and intra-psychic dynamics that, if understood, can open up the possibility of relating from a different standpoint.

Shelley and Maria broke up with one another after five years. After a passionate six months at the beginning of their relationship things started to go wrong. Maria distanced herself from Shelley, who then felt insecure and pursued Maria, demanding that she not retreat. Meanwhile Maria became ill. Part of her illness was expressed in irascibility towards Shelley. She became enraged and threatening when Shelley tried to talk to her about their relationship, about how scared she felt and how emotionally alone she was. Shelley nursed and cared for Maria during her illness but found herself on the receiving end of Maria's depression and distress. Maria, herself guilty about being so needy, couldn't acknowledge the care and love she was receiving. She was desperately worried about her health and couldn't bear to find herself so openly helpless.

When they broke up, Shelley alternated between feeling guilty for having abandoned Maria, for not understanding her better, for perhaps causing her illness and feeling aggrieved that Maria had exploited her caring and failed to reciprocate emotionally. Maria for her part felt that her love was always being undermined, that Shelley made her feel she wasn't good enough, that Shelley was too grabby and demanding.

The stories about their relationship are quite typical. Maria went on to another relationship where similar dynamics were played out; Shelley to one in which, in time, she became the withdrawn and pursued party. In this new relationship, Shelley felt invaded and harassed, and annoyed with her partner for not appreciating the love she was giving.

Shelley's experience of finding herself in Maria's shoes, so to speak, allowed her to rethink her story of her and Maria's break-up. She began to consider the ways in which she had been both active and acted upon in the relationship. It wasn't that Maria was simply a withdrawn, punishing, difficult and ill woman, nor was it that Shelley had pushed her away by her excessive neediness. She came to see that both of their insecurities had swamped their relationship, overshadowing their fears about intimacy, contact, need, commitment, personal space – issues they had needed to engage with as a couple.

Ellen, reaching retirement age, wanted to move out to the countryside, concentrate on her painting and gardening. Her children were grown up and her marriage to Mike, a man she respected but had gradually grown apart from, was reduced to infrequent companionship. She wanted to be on her own. She made plans to buy a cottage and to ease away from Mike without too much disruption. He could keep the family home and she would visit from time to time. But Mike, alarmed at losing both his just-married eldest daughter and his wife, became vicious and vindictive. Ellen had misperceived the enormous importance of the (to her eyes) limited contact Mike had had with her and their children. She felt he would be able to accept this arrangement as it only moved one step further than what seemed to her a *fait accompli*.

When Ellen planned to withdraw Mike panicked and became so scared that he immediately hitched up with another woman, cut himself off from Ellen and his children and tied their joint matters up in the divorce courts.

Several years later, Mike was transformed in Ellen's eyes into an ogre. What had started off as an attempt at an amicable separation initiated by her had been rewritten as a story in which he had wronged her. He had left her, run off and abandoned the family. Indeed Mike had done these things. In large part this was because in her threatened absence he became aware of his need and dependency on Ellen and the relationships she established for him both inside and outside the family. He wasn't a demonstrative or openly emotional man. He relied on Ellen to do the emotional relating.

But while Mike had participated in a very dramatic break-up, Ellen had meanwhile 'forgotten' that she had precipitated the divorce; that it was *she* who had wanted to disengage from the relationship. She turned herself into a victim and became quite unstable.

When her sister – fed up with the litany of victimisation – reminded Ellen that it had been she who had wanted to leave the relationship, Ellen knew that she was right. She began to reconstruct herself and the story she had been living by for several years. She recognised how fearful she had been about being direct with Mike about her own wishes and needs to separate and how her indirectness had contributed to a situation in which he, unable to contain his own anxiety, had boomeranged his rejected feelings back at her. When she could recognise this conflict she could rewrite the ending of her marriage. Reinserting her own agency reminded her of her own original wishes. She realised that her conflict about exposing what she wanted and her own fears about being on her own (even though she longed for that) had been buried even suppressed in the story of Mike 'that bastard'. Remembering her own desire and hesitancy allowed her to feel sadness about the end of the marriage and dissolved her feelings of victimisation.

If in reviewing our old break-ups (or our present ones, if we are in the midst of this painful process), we can hold on to our sense of doing as well as being done to; if we can recognise our personal difficulties with intimacy; the conflict we have between separateness and autonomy; the needs we bring for attachment as well as our fears of engulfment; our compulsion to replay and survive the emotional imprint of earlier significant relationships; our wish to rewrite our relationships in terms of good and bad; our desire to destroy what fails us and to mythologise what works, then we may be able to enter into new relationships with an awareness that such conflicts will surface and require attention. While we may transfer old conflicts to new relationships, perhaps we can avoid the situation where they smoulder awaiting a difficulty that shows us that old needs, far from being resolved, have simply been grafted on.

Women Observed

From early in life girls absorb the lesson of caution, of restraint, of fear, so that we come to be wary of our bodies. Our bodies are often invested with what appears as a negative strength – men will harm us, other women envy us.

Needs and Guilt

'Show me a woman who isn't guilty and I'll show you a man.' Although Erica Jong wrote this phrase well over a decade ago, guilt remains a disabling emotional response in many women's lives.

Guilt can be a perplexing and an uncomfortable feeling. Held inside the individual it corrodes good feelings. Expelled outside, it often confuses those who receive it. A woman may confess her infidelity to her husband. At a conscious level she does this out of a wish to be honest and to open up the issues that led her to sleep with someone else, but she also needs to unburden herself of uncomfortable guilt. Her husband has been unfaithful himself in the past but never disclosed his external liaisons. He now feels enraged and threatened. He physically attacks her and obsessively pursues her for details of the affair. She feels hounded but her guilt leads her to accept the terms on which he attacks her: she feels she has betrayed him and herself and so deserves to be punished.

Another woman spends a great deal of money shopping, concealing this from her partner. She feels great guilt and shame and is unable to disclose the difficulty she is in. Her shame leads her to withdraw from her partner, who feels the exclusion, becomes insecure and draws back from her. Her isolation leads her to feel even worse. She knows she is causing pain all around but trapped in her shame and guilt, she feels unable to do anything.

Guilt often erupts when we transgress some personal code, such as cheating, stealing, engaging in sexual betrayal or being unexpectedly cruel to another. In such circumstances, guilt may well be an appropriate emotional response. This kind of guilt indicates to us the hurt we have caused to ourselves.

Guilt alerts us to the importance of paying attention to the effects of an ill-conceived action. If we investigate it, we can find a way to accept our behaviour, to understand our actions and their implications rather than beating ourselves up inside or trying to relieve ourselves of the guilt by dumping it out. Behind this kind of guilt are important ways of understanding.

But often guilt arises in bewildering circumstances. The guilt seems unconnected to the action; or it seems too exaggerated a response for the imagined or real transgression. Particularly for women, guilt manifests itself in three ways. First, women often feel guilty when they are caught within the pincer movement of competing demands from others. The gender-linked psychological imperative of responding to others and being alert to their needs leads women to attend to the demands of others. But when there is no clear way to discern which of another's needs are most important, an excruciating paralysis can occur which gets cemented together with guilt feelings.

Secondly, linked to these paralysing feelings, but even more difficult to cope with, is the guilt that arises when an external demand competes with an internal desire. Because women are so used in their personal lives to deferring to others, individual needs can feel in and of themselves selfish. Although a woman may experience perfectly ordinary wishes, the internalised taboo on the acceptance of personal desire and personal need can be so strong that it induces feelings of greed, insatiability and confusion. The guilt is like a stopper on the original desire and it diverts the rage and confusion about why personal desire is so unacceptable into an attack on self and a punishment for even wanting. Guilt in this instance acts as a mechanism of conversion: it turns questions and anger into a blanket of self-suffocation.

Despite changes in their social roles, women's psychologies today still reflect what women have absorbed while growing up. The pressing attention to others' desires; the substitution of personal needs by meeting needs in others; the requisite of keeping tuned emotional antennae that can detect the requirements of others, limit a woman's capacity to feel happy with the existence of her own wants. Guilt becomes a silencer. When the taboo is broken through it acts as a brake on her desire, reminding the woman that it is not her place to want. Guilt scolds her and rebinds her nascent desire.

Because women have become reasonably accustomed to meeting personal needs indirectly, even though this is deeply unsatisfying, denial of these needs is often an important part of a woman's psychology. Guilt takes on many functions, binding up what are felt to be inappropriate or uncomfortable desires as well as demobilising women in the face of competing demands. The third way guilt operates is as an adhesive holding one to denial.

When a desire or an initiative asserts itself which is outside one's customary personal experience, there may be accompanying fear. Sarah wanted to leave her teenage children and husband for a week's holiday with a friend. But she discovered that she couldn't do it. She was unused to conceiving of herself as separate from them, and found herself in the grip of an extreme attack of guilt over her own wishes as well as her own anxieties. For her the guilt became a glue that kept her stuck to a situation that she knew.

Rachel was weary with listening to her elderly mother's constant complaints and acceding to her demands. She felt sorry for her, but also felt angry with her and with herself for not being able to change the situation. She felt herself to be very much her mother's mother. When she tried to pry herself loose, to detach herself from this position she was swamped by enormous guilt. She felt she was abandoning her mother. While part of her resented this bind, another part inserted herself into her mother's experience. She imagined her mother's loneliness, she felt her mother's helplessness, and this awareness fostered a guilt which kept her trapped into servicing her. She had the experience of being able to buoy her mother up; this combined with her guilt to hold her in the position of 'mothering' her mother.

When guilt acts as a brake on personal desire, when it acts to contain the individual, or when it represents a means of self-denial, it can be extremely paralysing. The person feels trapped and can't envisage a way out. If that guilt can be seen as a trap then questions can be asked about its function. In raising questions, we have the possibility of thinking about our options differently. If guilt is seen as the beginning of a response rather than the end point then it need not be so crippling. It can open up new ways of relating to entrenched patterns and ways of being.

The Power of the Feminine

It is true, as the writer and journalist Philip Norman writes in the *Guardian*, that men are bewildered by sex and by women. It's true too that women are bewildered by sex and by men. But does men's bewilderment mean we can fall into a set of warmed-up platitudes, or does it demand that we actually think through some of the fears that changes between the sexes are revealing?

Philip Norman's device of bringing in an overwhelmed zoologist to describe current relations between the sexes is flawed by its starting premiss. Zoologists observe animal behaviour that is repeated over time. Birds build the same kinds of nest; ants the same kinds of anthill, bees the same kinds of beehive. The point about human behaviour and human interaction is that we don't only build the same nest again and again. Indeed what distinguishes us from our animal cousins is our capacity to create new forms and thereby transform our conditions. We human beings are forever encountering new circumstances which affect us and on which we can have an impact. We have the capacity for intentionality and for self-consciousness, both as individuals and as a species.

There is nothing new about sexual relations being in flux.

Struggle and repositioning have characterised the arrangements between women and men from the turn of the century (and before, of course, but not so rapidly and not, until recently, affecting all social classes). What needs to be addressed now is the fear that is engendered by these changes.

Most women are afraid of and more or less interested in men, and most men are afraid of and more or less interested in women. What is *new* is that we are becoming more open about acknowledging our fears. Where contempt, rage, idealisation and bewilderment were often the pillars that supported women's expressed feelings towards men and paternalism, idealisation, confusion and aggression the pillars that supported men's expressed feelings towards women, we now seem more prepared to examine what is behind these sets of attitudes.

Sex, love, attachment, reproduction, the place in which women and men most palpably come together, has long been fraught. And a continuing lament through this history, a history written, painted and voiced largely by men is: 'What do women want?'

Today the lament has grown to an exasperated groan: 'What the hell do they want and how dare they wear short skirts and yet want to spurn sexual attention?' How dare we indeed. How dare we look sexual without being ready to fuck. How dare we contest the notion that there was a golden age of sexual liberation two decades ago. How dare we attempt to define and refine our understanding of relationship, of sexual encounter, of attachment. How dare we challenge the separation between private and public space. How dare we 'feminise' the culture?

What men's fear of women and their annoyance at women's flagrancy expresses is the difficulty all of us experience in trying to come to terms with the ambiguous status of the power of women. As men and women respond to the changes between the sexes in the external world, we do so with reference to the internal images we have of women. Our experience of the external world that all of us participate in is not only a rational experience. We don't see individual women as they are. Our experience of them is mediated by the ambiguous image of women's power which we have all internalised.

I say ambiguous because we all wrestle with the power of the feminine, the power of the individual mother who gave birth to us and raised us, who when we were little had the power to hurt or soothe. When we could let it be known that we were wanting, we relied upon her accurately to interpret those wants, to respect them and to try to meet them. If our needs were seen and not belittled, even if not necessarily answered, then we had the capacity to know that our needs – that is to say what arises out of us, the most personal aspects of who we are, the idiom through which we express ourselves – were fundamentally all right. We could continue to show ourselves and our wants directly and hope that we could be answered.

But if our needs were ridiculed or if, however ingeniously we attempted to communicate, we could not be heard and seen, we found ourselves in a state of formidable helplessness in relation to a woman. This helpless dependency – a helplessness that humanity finds intolerable – becomes twisted in two ways. Either one situates oneself as culpable, affirming the power of the feminine and rendering oneself as guilty, or that helplessness gets turned inside out. We deny the terms in which our experience is cast by engaging in acts of domination or the wish to dominate; by doing to others a version of what we feel has been done to us.

Thus, if instead of being able to take for granted the recognition from one's mother that allows one to live and act creatively, we find ourselves in a relation of longing, then the fear of domination is turned into the wish to dominate; the fear of annihilation into the wish to annihilate; the fear of being ignored into the wish to ignore; the fear of being disliked into the wish to dislike; the fear of being a trouble into the wish to be a trouble; the fear of compliance into the wish to command compliance, and so on. These transpositions of desire are felt most excruciatingly in that first significant relationship: the relation to mother, to a woman.

This struggle with a woman which lives inside each of us to some extent or another shapes our relationship to self throughout our lives. Boys and men find through their gender difference, through the taking up of masculine behaviour and activities, and through foisting on adult women a version of the power they felt their mothers held over them in infancy, a way to assuage the helplessness they felt in their original encounter with the feminine. But their sense of difference may be more ephemeral than solid. When the masculinity they have forged is tampered with by repeated buffeting from the demands of women as a group, and by structural changes which are depriving men of an important mainstay of identity in the form of work and sexual power, their hold on their masculinity may become too tenuous to be comfortable. Social changes may then be resisted, ridiculed or feared, for they echo the memory of helplessness.

For girls and women, the struggle to come to terms with the power of the mother is also profound. For while the internal image of mother is a strong one, the external, societal representation of the feminine is degraded. In establishing an identity girls must juggle these opposing images. We veer between disavowing that power and asserting our right to a power which is rarely sanctioned. We fear our own power as much as men's and we unwittingly collude and dissemble even while we fight to define it.

Yes indeed, the sexes are in great fear of one another. There is much to lose and much to gain. But blaming – as Philip Norman does – pleasingly dressed women of any age for our powerful conflictual feelings is surely part of the problem rather than part of the solution.

Our Fairy-Tale Princess

The Royals are Britain's movie stars. They've been used as the glue to mend our fragmented and distorted relationship to public culture. As the notion and reality of a cohesive community is promoted at the same time in history as a communal consensus is fast disappearing (if indeed there ever was one), we take what we are offered in the public sphere as a way to engage in being a nation. So we find ourselves forging an identification with the family that is meant to represent us, to mirror our aspirations, to bind together the disparate forces that make up modern Britain. And even though the Royals cannot do this, even though a stage-managed show like the House of Windsor fails to create any more than a cosmetic sense of community, our craving for it is so strong that it leads us – often against our conscious will – to comply with and assent to this pretence.

As our world gets larger and more impersonal, as political acts are carried out in our name but without our consent or consultation, we become seduced by the offer of a relationship with Royalty as a way to limit our experience of diminishment. We cling on to a fantasy to lessen our alienation and create the illusion of inclusion.

But when the most intimate activities and desires of Princess Diana are brought into this relationship, activities and desires that one can't imagine she sanctions being sold as the latest goody on offer in the market-place, then our sensibilities are offended. We've been exposed to the *Daily Mail*'s or the *Sunday Times*'s version of her private life and their gloating analysis of whys and wherefores.

Princess Diana has been made into an object. For a brief period she represented one part of the split projected on to all women as she symbolised goodness, caring, self-restraint, maternal fealty and devotion. She carried this projection while her ex-sister-in-law was the recipient of the other side of the split projection: the wild sexual woman who in allowing her own desire courts terrible danger and destruction. Both conceptions of woman speak to a profound powerlessness that women experience within the limited confines of the madonna and whore imagery.

So we are offended because we know that the public persona speaks only to part of the Princess's experience, and that hidden behind the routine objectification lives a living, breathing human being who is managing the split that all women feel to some degree in a public context that is terrifying.

But because the way out of powerlessness for many little girls is the taking up of the fantasy of becoming a princess we are also offended. As we identify with the hurt and abused heroines in the fairy stories of our childhood, we are offered the Prince as a way out of misery. For Diana's Prince allegedly so to fail her, and for that to be exposed in so scurrilous a manner, is chilling. While all couples have to work through and survive hard times to accommodate to the reality of relationship as opposed to the fairy tale of romance, our Royals are expected to maintain the fantasy, to deny the difficulty and despair that find a place in many a relationship.

We are told that Diana, like many women, has sought to resolve the conflicts, disappointments and upset about her life and her marriage by transposing the split between restraint and desire on to food.

214

It is here that I am offended as a psychotherapist. Because, as the details of Diana's distressing relationship to her body image are paraded through the tabloids in a sensationalist fashion, I am keenly aware of how deeply shameful and upsetting a woman with bulimia feels her relationship to food is. Having worked with women with eating problems now for over twenty years, I am aware too of how very important secrecy is to the individual involved in the distressing syndromes of anorexia and bulimia. One develops anorexia or bulimia precisely because one can't or daren't expose what are felt to be impermissible desires. Desire is so forbidden that even self-acknowledgement may be unendurable. The psychotherapist's job is to help the person encounter in themselves what it is they find so shameful about their desires and needs, and to help them accept them.

To see journalists exploit what is so many women's experience, rather than listen and discover why desire itself is felt to be so taboo, shames us as a culture.

The Hunger Without a Name

In New York City a fundraising event to celebrate ten years of The Women's Therapy Centre Institute attracted 800 people who came to hear speakers, enjoy entertainers and see the film *The Famine Within*, which focused on the continuing pain, distress and anger that women feel about body image and food problems. In 1993 the Women's Therapy Centre in London marked sixteen years as an outpatient clinic serving women of all backgrounds who seek a dignified response to emotional problems. Although the work of both centres focuses on gender-conscious psychoanalytic psychotherapy, both also widely known for the work they do in the specific area of food and body image problems – a central issue in many women's lives.

The essence of the day in New York was distilled in the most powerful part of the programme, the Speak-Out on Food and Body Distress. The speak-out has been a feature of feminist activities since the beginning of the second wave of the women's liberation movement in the late 1960s. In a public yet protected forum women in speak-outs across the United States have come, one after the other, to the microphone, to talk about the

217

hurt, the anger and the confusions that have beset individual people trying to make sense of the contradictory messages from the family, the education system and the legislature about the expectations, the possibilities, the internal and external demands that devolve upon a woman.

In opening this third speak-out sponsored by The Women's Therapy Centre Institute on Food and Body Distress, Gloria Steinem talked about her own problems with food; about growing up with fat parents and developing a fear of food in a culture obsessed with thinness; she spoke of her obese older sister who is now in a wheelchair, and of her own difficulty with keeping food in the house for fear that she would gorge on it. She spoke of succumbing to a binge, throwing out food, pouring detergent on it to make it inedible and then finding herself ferreting around in the rubbish bin to feed herself any uncontaminated bits to appease a perplexing hunger that had no name.

As women came to the microphone to testify about their avoidance of food, their fear of embracing it, the relationship between bingeing and experiences of incest, of eating until comatose to soothe themselves, of eating to stop emotional pain, their dislike of their bodies, their identification with those in rebellion in Los Angeles whose civil and economic deprivation spilled out last month into a binge of what has been denied them, as women in their mid-sixties testified to the continued indignity of feeling that their bodies were never all right and could never be, as women related their experiences of hanging over the toilet bowl to rid themselves of the food that they could not allow themselves to keep inside themselves, as woman after woman detailed the time, money and emotional investment in diet clubs and weight reduction schemes, as highly educated women exposed self-contempt at their adherence to the biddings of the beauty industry, it became obvious that what we were observing was an assault on women, and women's attempt to fight back.

This wasn't a new insight. The very first women's groups

that tried to politicise the whole issue twenty-two years ago resituated the personal, idiosyncratic problems of the individual group members and created out of them a new understanding and perspective on women's relationship to food and body image. From those groups we understood that we could read women's relationship to their bodies as a metaphor. It was women's language that, once decoded, could tell us about the interior lives of contemporary women in the West. And what we discovered pained and enraged us deeply. The suffering behind the casually remarked, 'No I can't have that, I'm too fat', 'I can't go out until I lose a stone', 'I was so depressed, I ate the whole loaf', told us about an internal struggle between restraint and entitlement, between desire and denial, between appetite and negation, between yearning and restriction, between wanting and inhibition, between freedom and enslavement, between private and public, between love and hatred.

But as we were discovering the buried lives of women, the hours women spent trying to fix themselves, as we were extending our understanding of women's relationship to food, to fat, to femininity, as we were challenging the invasion of our bodies, as we were understanding more and more about our receptivity to that invasion, we were coming up against something we didn't yet have the words for, but which looked and felt like an unconscious conspiracy. We were coming up against what today we would recognise as the backlash.

This backlash consisted of a new assault on women's bodies, minds, aspirations and desires. Collectivism was derided, competition extolled; in Britain Margaret Thatcher told us there was no such thing as society. It was our fault if our lives hurt, if the housing was rotten, the jobs corrupt and boring, the childcare provision non-existent, the food poisoned, the cities decaying . . . Rape, wife battering, violence against women increased and although women insisted that this violence reflected an unhealthy society, their protest was ridiculed. In Britain feminism was derided and became a dirty word.

Meanwhile, the woman in the advertisements got skinnier

and skinnier. She became Superwoman with an important job, a perfect child, a wonderful relationship and of course a body groomed for Hollywood: manicured, exercised, immaculate. We didn't recognise ourselves in these advertisements, yet we succumbed. We succumbed to the pressure to separate ourselves from one another; we succumbed to looking a certain way. Where for a fleeting moment in the 1970s we had set our own agenda, we began to pass again, to wax our legs, shave our armpits, colour our hair and worry about our size. Despite the evidence that many women were plagued with self-hatred, body hatred, insecurity and anger, the majority of women nevertheless had to contend with the backlash on their own. Our feminist aspirations were gutted and we were being sold back a package of femininity that we half recognised, that we half related to.

To reverse the backlash we have to re-socialise our experience. To recognise once again that one of the crippling requirements for contemporary femininity, wherever women are located on the class or cultural map, is an imperative of service, of giving, of midwifery, of doing for others. By seeing this, we understand that the psychological price of focusing on the needs of others can produce a discomfort with recognising one's own.

And we understand, too, how our bodies continue not to be our own. From early in life girls absorb the lesson of caution, of restraint, of fear. So much so that we come to be wary of our bodies, afraid of the trouble they'll get us into, while unsure of their strength. Our bodies are often invested with what appears as a negative strength – men will harm us, other women envy us. And yet we learn that these bodies, even today, are crucial to the outcome of our lives. If we are fat we risk attack or stigmatisation on the job. If we are fat we risk scorn and prejudice from the medical profession. If we are fat we are pitied. If we love women sexually we will be excluded from the culture, ridiculed and rubbished, told that what we need is . . . And of course our bodies come in different colours. If we are not white, we face racism. Our bodies are not just the wrong size but our physical features, the ratio of melanin to carotene, disturbs the sensibilities of the dominant class and we are discriminated against in the most obvious as well as the most subtle of ways.

The speak-out brought women together to repel the attack, to claim a space for themselves and their bodies, to weep and to laugh together as they shared their stories and those of the countless women who couldn't be there. It was a moving event and an inspiring day.

Liberty Takers

Sexual harassment is (according to the European Commission) the most common and least discussed occupational health hazard for women. It makes millions of women miserable every day, causes work absenteeism, depression and poor motivation . . . 51% of British women have suffered at some time in their working life.
(Christine Crawley, Chair of the European Parliament Women's Rights Committee)

The allegations of sexual harassment which emerged from Anita Hill's testimony in the United States Senate hearings to confirm the appointment of Clarence Thomas to the Supreme Court have brought choruses of recognition from women everywhere. Women have talked about their own experiences of being sexually harassed, about their identification with Anita Hill's long silence and about her bravery in testifying.

These women are from all walks of life. Their experiences are various. But they are able to imagine what Anita Hill went through and why she had been silent for so long. Their understanding has been at an emotional level as much as at a purely political level, which is to say that they have understood her through their own experiences of the humiliation, shame, outrage and hurt of sexual harassment. So how is this? How does such a widespread abusive practice become disregarded, trivialised, silenced, ridiculed or ignored as it did with Clarence Thomas's confirmation? How have women come to be so ashamed and confused about this form of invasion?

Of course these two questions are interrelated. As long as women are derided for making a fuss about being harassed, women will feel conflict about giving voice to their own experience. As long as women's voices are not heard on this subject, or heard as almost out of range, public attitudes will stay stuck in some facile and defensive response such as 'the spurned woman' or 'the asexual bitch'.

But still we need to explain the phenomenon that stops so many of us from making a fuss about sexual harassment at the time when it occurs. Three factors fold together here in such a way that for many many women protest, challenge or legal action seems almost impossible.

Without doubt the economic threat underpins women's silence. Women sense the cost of challenging a boss, a manager or even a co-worker who is pestering them with unwanted sexual advances. Their job may disappear or they may be marginalised or sneered at. While women increasingly win cases at industrial tribunals the process is barely known about. And at any rate, that is a route only for those women who have felt able to report, to testify, to withstand the pressure of the tabloids and the all too frequent disapproval of friends, co-workers, shop stewards and so on.

Linked to the economic threat is, of course, women's social position and the way in which women and men have come to regard women's sexuality. From early on in childhood, girls who are now adults absorbed the idea that they must be wary, even fearful, of their bodies and what they can do. We take in the idea that our sexuality is somehow dangerous – dangerous for ourselves and dangerous for men. At the same time we've learnt that our sexuality is our ticket to adulthood – until recently the only legitimate way for a woman to separate from her family of origin.

Sexual liberation may be a reality (although I doubt it) for girls growing up today, but it is a misnomer for adult women's experience. We may have fought to put our sexuality on the agenda, our sexual desire or lack of it, our sexual interests and so on, but the pervasive experience for many adult women is still that their sexual lives continue to be framed by what is possible within the external and internalised confines of patriarchy.

At the heart of these constraints is the fact that for many women, experience of their sexuality and of their bodies is confusing. Brought up to see our bodies as our productions, as the result, if you like, of the work we put into them, we anticipate and may even desire a certain level of sexual attention. What is problematic is the lack of control over that attention. The woman presents herself to the world with her set of meanings, but people project on to her assumptions that may be unwarranted and unwanted. In a world where women are designated as the sexual object for both sexes, presenting oneself in sexually attractive ways is indeed a route to garner some self-esteem. But this doesn't mean that women invite or wish for persistent sexual innuendo, touching or attention.

By the same account, women who dare to turn their back on presenting themselves in a 'sexual' manner do not invite the vicious intrusion implied in 'what you need is a good fuck' comments. Sexual harassment is part and parcel of a culture that locates sexuality outside of us, that sells sex as a commodity, that separates sex from relationship and uses it to make us feel enticed by the consumer goodies on offer. The economic and social strictures that press in on women create a particular shape to a feminine psychic structure. Combined, these factors make it possible to understand why women may find it extremely hard to speak up about harassment at the time when it happens.

Since she is brought up to believe that her desire should reflect the needs of others, a woman's capacity to trust her own voice, to regard her own experience as valid, is endangered.

We now know that many children have suffered silently through being sexually abused. That silence is the silence of the powerless victim who feels and knows something is wrong but who has no one to turn to; who has no words to speak that can communicate the hurt, the wrong, the mistreatment; who has little hope that the situation will change. So too with sexual harassment. The woman at first wonders whether she misconstrues the situation. Did she imagine it, perhaps? It continues and she protests. But her protest is ignored, the unwelcome attention continues and may be stepped up. She feels a mixture of things – outrage, violation, confusion, pity. She tells a friend or a co-worker. Perhaps they tell her she is exaggerating, is making too much of it, so she feels invalidated in her response to the harassment. Perhaps she *is* making too much of it; after all, if she'd fancied the bloke, she wouldn't have minded his attention. Maybe she should try to pacify him. Be nice. No, that doesn't work; that seems to encourage him. Better try to keep her distance. Be polite and firm but tell him how uneasy it makes her.

Inside herself, she feels victimised by the situation and victimised by her own response. Why can't she just leave, hit him, report him, ignore him? She feels completely unsupported, helpless and devises strategies designed to change his behaviour. She becomes the culpable one. She must find the solution. Her failure to do so makes her feel bad. Add this to the distress caused by the humiliation of having one's body parts described in detail, squeezed or commented on and the woman is economically, socially and psychologically trapped.

Yes, it is easy to understand why Anita Hill and countless millions (yes millions) bear the pain of sexual harassment in silence for so long. But sexual harassment is finally on the agenda. For now we see it being derided in the US Senate decision just as it is in the individual workplace. The confirmation of Clarence Thomas condones in the public sphere what happens in individual offices.

But the space that has been opened up for women to talk about this is growing. Where there was silence and shame, we have seen dignity and bravery. Women are finding the words and the actions that will allow them to contest this reflexive behaviour and make sexual harassment the cause not of ridicule but of deep censure.

Hunger Strike

Joanna Clinton Davies's BBC TV *Forty Minutes* film on the treatment of adolescent anorectics at Dr Dee Dawson's Rhodes Farm lets us know something of the emotional struggle that leads these young people to consistently refuse food to the point of starvation. One teenager feels ousted by her new stepfather; another feels ignored in parental disputes; another struggles for control with parents who want her to ingest soft drinks rather than plain water; another's cycling habits (70 miles on a Sunday) seem to echo her father's interest in competitive sports; and the only anorectic male in residence tells of his deep self-hatred. The avoidance of food which these young people took as the solution to their problems is challenged in a warm, homey context in which, in a 'no nonsense' approach, Dr Dawson expects them to hand over control to her, accept that their experiences are distorted by chemical imbalances induced by voluntary self-starvation and to eat rich foods which will allow them to put on a minimum of 2 kilograms a week until they reach the target weight determined by a medical team.

Dr Dawson becomes the parental stand-in who, by providing clear boundaries and assuming benign control, relieves the

229

children of the burden of trying to fix their parents and instead get on with growing up. She provides, in part, a reparative experience for the children, who need to feel not so responsible for others' lives, who need attention to their emotional problems, and who need to know that what they are doing by not eating may be worrying but that it doesn't frighten, overwhelm or awe others. Dee Dawson refuses to be frightened by these adolescents, and her relaxed lack of fear adds greatly to their ability to feel safe and trust her.

Unfortunately the adolescents in the documentary reinforced almost every possible prejudice that pervades our perception of anorexia nervosa. With the exception of one returnee there for advice, all the current residents were middle class and white. Their academic success was paraded as paradigmatic and they were repeatedly described by Dr Dawson as manipulative and as having a predisposition to anorexia. One could be left with feeling that anorexia was somehow an enigmatic yet genetic condition, curable by caring and the loading on of spoonfuls of calories.

But we now know that this isn't so, that the prejudices surrounding anorexia nervosa are simply prejudices. The experience of anorexia, of self-starvation, is not a manipulative act but a desperate attempt at a (false) solution to a set of interpersonal, intra-psychic and social problems. Those us of exposed to someone whose means of survival revolves around controlling what enters and what doesn't enter their body can feel frightened. We can and do feel manipulated and manoeuvred into a difficult position. But to equate what we feel when in their company with what is going on for them is to confuse a personal response with what is required in a clinical judgement.

Skilled clinicians take for granted that the anorectic can't but act in the way that she (and it is overwhelmingly she) is acting. The point is not to label the person but to get behind the meaning of the behaviour, to understand the terror that leads to the need to control her food and her emotional environment so drastically.

The phenomenon of course is not confined to the exam-passing middle classes. Anorexia hits all age groups and all social and ethnic groupings. While class and ethnic position may well determine access to treatment, clinical experience here and in the United States shows a significant incidence of anorexia nervosa in all groupings. Like the diagnosis of hysteria over a hundred years ago, we see in the present situation a 'disease' entity created for one group of people to the exclusion of the others.

Anorexia nervosa has been seriously on the increase in the last two decades and its rise in adolescents parallels a rise in body preoccupation in young girls and women in general. A recent British study confirms North American research which shows that 9-year-old girls are concerned with body image issues and that a significant proportion are already restricting their food intake. Why children are absorbing early on the message of restraint and body preoccupation, so much the bane of adult femininity, is what should concern us. We need to understand why young girls and adolescents find psychological survival in refusing food; why the passage to adulthood must be marked by body self-hatred and transformation, control and fear of food. We need to engage with the experience of the person in the grip of anorexia and help them to find other ways of expressing their fears and their pain which will eventually allow them to be relieved of that pain rather than concentrating on controlling their food.

Anyone who watched the *Forty Minutes* programme would have been struck by the paradox of Dr Dawson restricting her own children's intake of chocolate while foisting it on her residents. And they would not have missed her baleful comments about her own failed dieting. The unarticulated links between a culture of dieting and the setting of excessively calorie-rich foods before her charges were painfully visible.

Anorexia is a serious mental and physical problem. But it is also on a continuum with most women's experience of using and 'abusing' food. In the anorectic we are seeing the exaggeration of a response that is common in literally millions of women: the shocking social phenomenon that many women do not feel entitled to eat without guilt. We must try to come to grips with this. We must endeavour to understand how girls and women have internalised a sense that eating is for others and not for themselves. We must try to comprehend what is going on in the heart and mind of a woman who is engaged in voluntary starvation.

A hunger strike, which is, after all, what is at work in anorexia, is an act of the most extraordinary courage and the most extraordinary despair. Unless we face the fact of the hunger strike, until we decipher its aims, commit ourselves to understanding what cause the anorectic is fighting for, what conflicts, problems, worries, terrors and anxieties the anorexia is attempting to bind up, we cannot expect the symptom to abate. Until we can help her find other equally meaningful sources of strength and self-respect she will continue to tell us with her body what she is unable to speak about with her voice.

The Age of Dignity

To talk of the menopause, to talk of women and ageing, is to bring ridicule and embarrassment to 'polite' conversation. As Germaine Greer graphically demonstrated in *The Change*, menopausal women have been ravaged over the last hundred years. They've been operated on, bled, institutionalised, seen as mad or pathetic, or ignored and trivialised.

In our time too stereotypes predominate. We have on the one hand, the woman suffering from 'empty nest syndrome', psychology's soft term for the menopausal woman. It is she who is depicted in the pharmaceutical advertisements in medical magazines. She is depressed, life seems to have left her. Her children have grown up, her sexual powers have waned, her husband has lost interest in her and life without its reproductive and allied social functions is effectively over.

The other side of women's experience of this age is that they become invisible unless recast in the terms of the femininity that our culture values despite twenty-odd years of feminism. Joan Collins or Jane Fonda or Tina Turner can be visible because in their differing ways they refuse old age and create themselves either in the image of youth or in terms of a palpable sexuality.

While ageing women may be making enormous contributions to the culture, they have been denied the dignity and appreciation that would allow women in their fifties to celebrate their achievements, express their desires and go on to the next period of their lives with honour and status.

Now, as the generation of women who fought for the right to be heard on their own terms, in their own language, using their own definitions are becoming middle-aged, menopausal and post-menopausal, we can expect that a rich set of narratives will emerge about this experience that both describes and critiques our existing prejudices about women of a certain age.

Behind the clichéd notion of the depressed victim, we might expect to hear stories of a more complex nature. In the psychotherapist's consulting room the women I encounter struggling to understand their experience at 50 or so defies trite description. Of course these women have sought psychotherapy to alleviate the distress they are in and cannot stand in for the great body of individual experience that exists. Nevertheless it is interesting to know that for some menopause is not an issue, or to put it more accurately, it is not the issue around which other themes crystallise. Biological changes produce considerable trouble in some and not in others but for some the material being worked on in therapy (while reflecting the woman's age and experience of the world) is not defined by reference to the menopause.

For others, the menopause sets the frame for understanding a whole range of feelings, desires and confusions. Themes from childhood, adolescence and young adulthood reappear to be worked through again at a different level. A woman in her fifties who grew up feeling ashamed of her body, frightened by her sexual responses and warned that the power of her sexuality could cause havoc in her life and the lives of others, found adulthood a perplexing time. She came of age when sexual mores demanded that female sexuality be both constrained and exhibited but not accessible to her. Her ability to create out of herself a sexually attractive persona became part of her ticket to relationships. But *her* sexuality was uneasy. Unwanted pregnancy and the culturally engendered dirtiness of female sexuality were imprinted on her, making it extremely difficult for her to celebrate or express her sexuality.

Then in her late twenties the so-called sexual revolution came along just a bit too late. Despite the work of sexologists Masters and Johnson, despite the new prominence given to the clitoris, the chance to explore this aspect of herself bred (moral and psychological) confusion and fear. Her lack of entitlement to her body and her sexuality left her scared of her own body and fearful of her children's sexuality. So what menopause means to this woman is indeed a break from having to create herself in a particular image.

Since women are meant to be invisible when they are no longer recognisably sexual (i.e. youthfully sexual), she hides behind this cultural cloak and develops and explores aspects of self that she was uneasy with before. She becomes 'selfish'. She puts herself and her desires forward. She has bided her time through the last thirty years and now she is determined to live; to initiate on her own behalf; to put considerable energy into struggling through deeply internalised taboos and restraints. No one looks at her and she need no longer serve. The extensive effort expended on others is now turned inwards and she uses this time to connect herself with personal desire that she had long forgotten how to listen for. She creates her own mirror for self-confirmation, reflections that are internal rather than externally prescribed.

But what of the woman, heterosexually or homosexually inclined, who is coming upon the menopause and who has chosen not to reproduce? What does the cessation of menses mean to her? The responses are as varied as the women. For one woman it has meant a time of consolidation of earlier decisions. Her decision not to have babies is once again confirmed. For another, unexpected feelings of grief and loss confront her. The babies she chose not to have are now no longer her choice. She followed what was right for her but aches again over what was the correct but nevertheless conflictual decision she made many years ago.

Perhaps the cruellest experiences are reserved for those women who wanted to but couldn't reproduce, who feel again the anguish of wishes not granted while recognising the bittersweet relief of that possibility finally closing.

But the important thing is that we need to avoid characterising women in this period of their lives in the same limited ways that they have been characterised before. There aren't just two responses to the menopause ('She sailed through it' or 'It was the worst time of her life') or even just the four that I have outlined here. There are a myriad of idiosyncratic responses which encompass emotions ranging from mourning, to fear to liberation.

We are unused to a definition of womanhood that doesn't conform in some way to the limited view we as a culture have held of women. When we try to banish that view, or rather to expand, to allow into our picture of woman, of femininity, of the female, both the suffering that individual women have experienced and the challenges and chances individuals have taken, we find that we can no longer fit the woman into a box. She becomes visible in ways that defy our expectations and challenge the comfortable pigeon-holes (asexual, motherly, efficient, matronly, past it) we have assigned her and us.

After menopause there can well be another thirty years of life to live. The question is how to live it with dignity and respect and how to create a cultural climate that will honour and value women in all their variety and in all their ages.

Notes

The Victim Inside the Bully
Andy Metcalf's film, *Dot, Top Men and the Joeys*, was shown on BBC2 on 1 August 1993.

Emotional Responsibility
Mental Illness: The Fundamental Facts is available from the Mental Health Foundation, 37 Mortimer Street, London W1N 7RJ. £4.50.

NewPin, which stands for New Parent Infant Network, is a self-help initiative offering support to women experiencing difficulty with, and in some cases in danger of abusing, their young children. Sutherland House, Sutherland Square, Walworth, London SE17 3EE. Tel: 071 703 2660.

Christmas
Families and How to Survive Them (Methuen, London, 1983) by John Cleese and my colleague Robin Skynner is a book to read before Christmas in order to remind you of what you are up against.

Similarly no family with (young) children should consider being without *How To Talk So Kids Will Listen & Listen So Kids*

Will Talk by Adele Faber and Elaine Mazlish (Avon, New York, 1982). We at home read it twice a year. Leave it by the loo: it could change your daily life. Its presentation of emotionally literate parent–child relating can be applied to wider relationships.

Denial

The Women's Therapy Centre runs a one-year part-time course for women counsellors and psychotherapists working with women. Information from the WTC, 6 Manor Gardens, London N7 6LA.

Betrayal

Directory of Member Organisations, the United Kingdom Council for psychotherapy, Regent's College, Regent's Park, London NW1 4NS. £5.

1993 Counselling & Psychotherapy Resources Directory, the British Association of Counsellors, 1 Regent Place, Rugby CV21 2PJ. £22.

POPAN, 20 Daleham Gardens, London NW3 5DA.

Individual Psychotherapy Trainings: A Guide, by Jan Abram, Free Association Books, London. £17.95.

The Stiff Heart

Exploring Parenthood, Latimer Education Centre, Freston Rd, London W10. Tel: 081-960 1678.

Lost Boys and Absent Fathers

Janna Letts's moving television programme, *Lost Boys*, was shown on BBC1 on Sunday, 29 November 1992.

Robert Bly, *Iron John: A Book about Men*, Element Books, London, 1991.

Seriously Sexy

The videos produced by the Terence Higgins Trust are now on sale.

Violent Connections

The Women's Therapy Centre runs courses for practitioners working with abused women. For further information write to WTC, 6 Manor Gardens, London N7 6LA.

The Power of the Feminine
Philip Norman, 'Sex and Masculinity in the 90s', *Guardian*, 24 July 1993.

The Hunger Without a Name
The Famine Within, dir. Katherine Gilday for Canadian Broadcasting Corporation, 1991.
Susie Orbach, *Fat is a Feminist Issue* (Arrow Books, London, 1978).

Liberty Takers
Women Against Sexual Harassment (WASH), 242 Pentonville Road, London N1. Tel: 081-833 0222.

Hunger Strike
Joanna Clinton Davies's film, 'I Won't, I Can't' (*Forty Minutes*), was shown on BBC2 on 23 February, 1993.
A new edition of Susie Orbach's book *Hunger Strike* has been published (Penguin, Harmondsworth).

The Age of Dignity
Germaine Greer, *The Change: Women, Ageing and the Menopause*, Hamish Hamilton, London, 1991.
Rosetta Reitz, *Menopause: A Positive Approach*, Harvester Press, Brighton, 1978.
The Boston Women's Health Collective and Jean Shapiro, *Ourselves Growing Older*, Fontana, London, 1990.

Now you can order superb titles directly from Virago

☐	Bullying at Work	Andrea Adams	£8.99
☐	The Drama of Being a Child	Alice Miller	£7.99
☐	Torn in Two	Roszika Parker	£12.99
☐	The Female Malady	Elaine Showalter	£9.99
☐	Talking from 9 to 5	Deborah Tannen	£8.99
☐	The Argument Culture	Deborah Tannen	£16.99
☐	Slow Motion	Lynne Segal	£8.99
☐	My Father's House	Sylvia Fraser	£7.99

Please allow for postage and packing: **Free UK delivery.**
Europe; add 25% of retail price; Rest of World; 45% of retail price.

To order any of the above or any other Virago titles, please call our credit card orderline or fill in this coupon and send/fax it to:

Virago, 250 Western Avenue, London, W3 6XZ, UK.
Fax 0181 324 5678   Telephone 0181 324 5516

☐ I enclose a UK bank cheque made payable to Virago for £ ....

☐ Please charge £.............. to my Access, Visa, Delta, Switch Card No.

☐☐☐☐☐☐☐☐☐☐☐☐☐☐☐☐☐☐☐

Expiry Date ☐☐☐☐   Switch Issue No. ☐☐

NAME (Block letters please) ....

ADDRESS ....

....

....

Postcode ....Telephone ....

Signature ....

Please allow 28 days for delivery within the UK. Offer subject to price and availability.

Please do not send any further mailings from companies carefully selected by Virago ☐